Newman on Tradition

Newman's outline of his sermon "On Tradition",
10 July 1849 (see Appendix, pp. 172–3)

NEWMAN
ON
TRADITION

GÜNTER BIEMER

Translated and edited by
Kevin Smyth

HERDER AND HERDER

1967

HERDER AND HERDER NEW YORK

232 Madison Avenue, New York, N.Y. 10016

Revised version of the original German edition
"Überlieferung und Offenbarung. Die Lehre von der Tradition nach
John Henry Newman"
("Die Überlieferung in der neueren Theologie", edited by
Josef Rupert Geiselmann, vol. IV)
Herder, Freiburg, 1961

Nihil Obstat: Joannes M. T. Barton, S.T.D., L.S.S.
Censor deputatus

Imprimatur: ✠ Patritius Casey, Vic. Gen.
Westmonasterii, die 25a Aprilis, 1966

Library of Congress Catalog Card No. 66–21076
First printed in West Germany © 1967, Herder KG
Printed in the Republic of Ireland by Cahill & Co. Ltd.

To the

Professors

of

Duquesne University,

Pittsburgh,

at whose kind invitation

I taught there

in

1964

CONTENTS

ABBREVIATIONS xi

FOREWORD by Monsignor H. Francis Davis . . xv

AUTHOR'S PREFACE xviii

INTRODUCTION 1

PART ONE

Tradition in Anglican Theology from the 16th to the
19th Century 5

1. *The problem of tradition according to the Anglican
   theologians of the 16th to the 18th century* . . 7

   a) *The place of sacred scripture* . . . 7
   b) *Tradition as source of faith* . . . 12
   c) *The significance of the Apostles' Creed* . . 16
   d) *Church and infallibility* 19

2. *Tradition in Anglican theology in the first half of the
   19th century* 24

CONTENTS

PART TWO

The Historical Development of Newman's Views . 33

1. *Newman's early acquaintance with scripture* . . 33
2. *The theologians of Oriel and the principle of tradition* 36
3. *Newman and tradition during the Oxford movement* 42
4. *The breakthrough to the notion of development* . 48
5. *Newman and tradition after 1845* . . . 57

PART THREE

The Systematic Structure of Newman's Doctrine of Tradition 69

I. INTRODUCTION 69

II. THE "SACRAMENTAL" WORD 70

   1. *The going forth from God* . . . 70
   2. *Divine providence* 72
   3. *The work of the Holy Spirit* . . . 75

III. THE WORD IN THE WORLD 80

   1. *The heathens* 80
   2. *The Israelites* 84
   3. *Christians* 87
     a) *The orthodox* 87
     b) *Heretics* 89

IV. THE TRADITION OF THE WORD OF REVELATION
IN THE CHURCH 92

1. The faith handed on 93

a) The deposit 93
b) The Creed 95
c) Dogmatic definitions 98

2. The organs of tradition in the Church . 99

a) The teaching Church . . . 99

(i) The Apostles 99
(ii) The bishops 102
(iii) The councils 104
(iv) The papacy 105

b) The Church that is taught . . . 112
c) The law of testimony in the Church . 114

3. The modes of tradition 121

a) The divine idea 121
b) Being and becoming 126
c) Correct developmemt 130
d) The work of Antichrist . . . 135

V. DEFINITION OF TRADITION 138

1. A specific difficulty in the definition . . 138

2. The formal aspects 140

3. The material aspects 143

a) The life of the Church . . . 143
b) The conscience of the Church . . 145

CONTENTS

VI. SCRIPTURE AND TRADITION 149

    1. *The problem of the canon* 150

    2. *The inspiration of scripture* . . . 152

    3. *The interpretation of scripture* . . . 154

        a) *The imperfection of its language* . . 154
        b) *The structure of scripture* . . . 155
        c) *The mystical sense* 156

    4. *Tradition as interpreter of scripture* . . 158

    5. *Scripture as guardian of tradition* . . 160

    6. *The question of the sufficiency of scripture* . 161

        a) *The whole of revelation in scripture* . 161
        b) *Living tradition in relation to scripture* . 163

CONCLUSION 167

APPENDIX: Manuscripts of Newman on Tradition . 171

SELECT BIBLIOGRAPHY 193

INDEX OF NAMES 205

ABBREVIATIONS

AAS	*Acta Apostolicae Sedis*
Apologia	*Apologia pro Vita Sua*
Arians	*The Arians of the Fourth Century*
A.V.	*Authorized Version*
Catholic Sermons	*Catholic Sermons of Cardinal Newman*
Denzinger	H. Denzinger, *Enchiridion Symbolorum*
Discourses	*Discourses Addressed to Mixed Congregations*
Discussions	*Discussions and Arguments on Various Subjects*
DNB	*Dictionary of National Biography*
Essays Critical	*Essays Critical and Historical*
Essay on Development	*Essay on the Development of Christian Doctrine*

Fifteen Sermons	*Fifteen Sermons Preached before the University of Oxford*
Grammar of Assent	*An Essay in Aid of a Grammar of Assent*
Jager	J. N. Jager, *Le Protestantisme aux prises avec la doctrine catholique*
JTS	*Journal of Theological Studies*, Oxford
Justification	*Lectures on Justification*
Lectures on Difficulties	*Lectures on Certain Difficulties felt by Anglicans in Catholic Teaching*
Meditations	*Meditations and Devotions*
Miracles	*Two Essays on Biblical and on Ecclesiastical Miracles*
Mozley	A. Mozley, *Letters and Correspondence of John Henry Newman during his life in the Anglican Church*
MS	Manuscripts of J. H. Newman, dealing with Tradition, from the Newman Archives in the Oratory, Birmingham
Newman-Keble Correspondence	*Correspondence of John Henry Newman with John Keble and Others*
Newman-Studien	*Kardinal Newman-Studien*

xii

Occasional Sermons	*Sermons Preached on Various Occasions*
ODCC	*Oxford Dictionary of the Christian Church*
Office	*The Office of the Holy Ghost under the Gospel*
Parochial Sermons	*Parochial and Plain Sermons*, I–VIII
Perrone	G. Perrone, *Praelectiones Theologicae*, I–IX
Present Position of Catholics	*Lectures on the Present Position of Catholics in England*
Przywara-Karrer	J. H. Kardinal Newman, *Christentum. Ein Aufbau,* I–VIII, ed. and translated by E. Przywara and O. Karrer
Sermon Notes	*Sermon Notes of John Henry Cardinal Newman*
Subjects of the Day	*Sermons Bearing on Subjects of the Day*
Tracts Theological	*Tracts Theological and Ecclesiastical*
M. Ward	Maisie Ward, *Young Mr. Newman*
W. Ward	Wilfrid Ward, *The Life of John Henry Cardinal Newman,* I–II

FOREWORD

WHENEVER A new theological insight captures the mind
and imagination of a new generation of theologians,
sooner or later, indeed sooner rather than later, some
Newmanist appears in print to tell us all that John Henry
Newman saw this and said this over a hundred years ago.
This has been said during Vatican Council II of many such
insights. People are no longer greatly surprised. They
shrug their shoulders and make some such remark as:
"This is just another sign that he was a century ahead of his
contemporaries".

He would be the first to correct us, if we thought that
these insights were totally new discoveries. To be true
insights, if they are Christian, they must already be
implicit in the Christianity of every age. The reason why
they suddenly come to be seen in a new light, and seen to
be in a new way important and vital for our age, is
because such new insights are always the result of a return
to the Christian sources, combined with a deepening of
spiritual life and an effort to make that life more authentic.

This explains to a great extent why Newman anticipated such developments. The reason why his approach to Christian revelation was always authentic was that it was never purely abstract. It was always bound up with his own life. When he "discovered" the importance of the notion of the development of Christian doctrine, it was because, at the time he wrote, only this theory made it possible for him to continue to live authentically as a Christian,—or so it appeared to him. If he wrote on the assent to faith, it was part of a desperate effort to reach the millions who fail to arrive at faith through a misunderstanding of what it involves and of what is asked of them.

The same is true of the subject of this important monograph. Tradition for Newman was not just a theological concept. It was the Word of God in our midst, bringing us eternal life, now as at all other times in Christian history. It involved the real presence of the Holy Spirit and our response to that Spirit. Some understanding of Divine Tradition, Newman saw, was bound up with the very process of being a Christian, provided Christianity was real. Do we, or do we not, live by the word of God in scripture? How is this word that comes to us in scripture related to the word of God handed down to us by word of mouth? How is it related to the creeds we were taught, and teach our children? Has our faith its roots in scripture? Is it all on the surface of scripture?

Newman could not have continued to live as a Christian without answering such questions. His answer is strikingly similar to that of the majority of the theologians of Vatican II.

Even on the most modern of questions one never fails to profit by the characteristic approach of Newman's genius and spirituality. Some of us feel we detect here the reflections of holiness.

Dr. Biemer speaks kindly of me. I wish his words were fully merited. These words at least indicate to the reader that we have long been closely associated. I have immense pleasure in being able to introduce to the English-speaking public his first book in our language. When you have read and studied it, you will, like myself, hope and pray that it will be the first of many from his fruitful pen.

H. FRANCIS DAVIS

Birmingham,
May 10th, 1966.

AUTHOR'S PREFACE

IN TODAY'S Newman studies, the present book occupies an intermediate position between the presentation of his work on the development of dogma and that of his teaching on sacred scripture. The effort here made to assess comprehensively and systematically Newman's attitude to tradition was inspired by an essay of Heinrich Fries on the subject, "Newmans Beitrag zum Verständnis der Tradition", which appeared in a more general work on oral tradition, M. Schmaus, ed., *Die mündliche Überlieferung* (1957), pp. 63–122. It is undoubtedly surprising that in spite of all the work that has been done on Newman's doctrine, no effort has been made to give a full and adequate treatment of the place of tradition in his life and writings (an approach from the point of view of the doctrine of development is made by J. H. Walgrave in the first part of his work, *Newman. Le développement du dogme*, 1957), though the Cardinal himself was the first to point out that it was decisive: "The Fathers made me a Catholic" (*Lectures on Certain Difficulties felt by Anglicans in Catholic*

Teaching, II, p. 24). The reason for the comparative neglect of so central a question may perhaps be indeed that the sweep of the theological and philosophical genius of Newman hardly seems to offer a sharply-defined and systematic contribution to the theme. Painstaking study of details is needed before it becomes apparent that the notion of tradition is to some extent directive in all his writings, and indeed that his whole life may be said to revolve around it. These findings are confirmed above all by the hitherto unpublished texts from the rich Newman archives at Birmingham, and the relevant texts are put before the reader as far as is possible, partly in the notes and partly in the appendix to this book.

The arrangement and presentation of the matter was determined throughout by the nature of the sources. But the peculiar course of Newman's life was also taken into account, as well as his own wish to have his doctrine available some time or other in a systematic form. And since neither the theology of Newman in general nor his teaching on tradition in particular can be properly understood except against the background of Anglican theology, it was necessary to give some idea of it, in so far as it affected Newman's starting-point. Hence the pages devoted to the great names in Anglican theology.

I take this opportunity of expressing my thanks to Dr Heinrich Fries, formerly professor at Tübingen and now at Munich University, to whom, as the leading authority on Newman in Germany, and my own respected teacher, I owe the encouragement and benevolent interest which have accompanied this book from the start.

I am also very glad to thank here my teacher and friend, Mgr Henry Francis Davis, at whose lectures in the Northcote Hall of Oscott College I heard, in 1952 and 1953, what were for me the decisive words about Newman. As Vicepostulator of the cause of Newman's beatification, Mgr Davis must now be considered as the leading Newman scholar, since the death of Fr Henry Tristram. In England too I must acknowledge my debt to Fr C. Stephen Dessain, now head of the Oratory at Edgbaston where Newman was once superior. As guardian of the precious Newman archives, he generously provided me with the fullest facilities during my four months' study of the manuscripts.

For the English edition this study has remained unchanged in its results as originally published in German in 1961. However, the Introduction and Part Two, "The Historical Development of Newman's Views", have been completely rewritten and compressed in order to show more precisely the decisive stages in Newman's approach to the problem. I am deeply indebted to Mr Kevin Smyth for his excellent translation as well as for having edited the book so well.

As the work of adapting the original study for its publication in English has been done by me here in Pittsburgh, Pa., where I have been lecturing and holding a seminar on "Newman and Ecumenism" as Visiting Professor of Theology at Duquesne University, I have great pleasure in dedicating this edition to the staff of Duquesne University.

Pittsburgh, Pa.,   Günter Biemer
Easter 1964.

Introduction

THE NINETEENTH century can be called the century of tradition in many regards, both in the history of culture and of Christian theology. It includes extremist trends, one-sided views and cautious pioneering steps. Efforts were made to return to the past at all levels, but by over-simplifying the problems, as was the case in the mistaken efforts of traditionalism. But there were also fruitful innovations, as in the case of the understanding of tradition put forward in the Tübingen school of Catholic theology.

The Anglican Church of the nineteenth century was also strongly affected by this effort at a renewal that would come to terms with the traditional. The forces at work were embodied in the leading theologians of the Oxford Movement,[1] launched and guided by John Henry Newman. Its aim was to establish the validity of their Church

---

[1] Cf. G. Biemer, "Oxfordbewegung" in *Lexikon für Theologie und Kirche* (2nd ed., 1957–1965), VII, col. 1323–4.

for present and for future times by demonstrating how well it was rooted in its apostolic foundation.

Newman is of particular importance in this connexion. His reflections on revelation as the legacy of the Apostles, as truth transmitted to be preserved and handed on, brought up the problem of faith in the form of tradiition with the question of how the historical nature of tradition affected the transmission of the doctrine of Jesus Christ.

The present work begins with an attempt to give a survey of Newman's own life as he confronted the reality and the notion of the tradition of revelation.[2] Before giving the history of his problem, however, we shall give an outline, brief and therefore limited, but nonetheless valid, of the Anglican notion of scripture and tradition as source of faith.[3] Its real aim will be to give a clear and definite picture of Newman's first position and his later attitudes in the light of his original background.

The following section will try to give a full and systematic exposition of Newman's doctrine of tradition. Since Newman never wrote a special treatise on the subject and since his views developed in depth and precision in the course of his life, our effort here to give systematic structure to his thought, which sometimes remained at the stage of preliminary essays and outlines of future expansion, can only be tentative.

[2] The historical section is more fully treated in the dissertation on which this translation is based, Günter Biemer, *Überlieferung und Offenbarung. Die Lehre von der Tradition nach John Henry Newman* (1961).
[3] Cf. G. H. Tavard, *Holy Writ or Holy Church. The Crisis of the Protestant Reformation* (1959) and *The Quest for Catholicity* (1964).

Similar efforts have already been made by students of Newman. The following study is on the same lines and acknowledges its debt to them. Jaak Seynaeve has given a comprehensive presentation of *Newman's Doctrine on Holy Scripture* (1953). More recently, Jean Henri Walgrave has investigated the doctrine of development in his *Newman the Theologian* (1964). Newman's doctrine on the Church has been examined from different points of view by W. H. van der Pol[4] and Norbert Schiffers.[5] His doctrine on tradition has already been treated in an essay by Heinrich Fries.[6]

In the context of these works on "fundamental theology", the present study will try to make available to present-day theology a further contribution of Newman's thought.

---

[4] *Die Kirche im Leben und Denken Newmans* (1937).
[5] *Die Einheit der Kirche nach John Henry Newman* (1956).
[6] See Author's Preface.

PART ONE

Tradition in Anglican Theology from the 16th to the 19th Century

It is impossible to do any sort of justice to Anglican doctrine, as mirrored by representative Anglican theologians, without keeping two essential difficulties in mind, which must be noted at the very beginning. We are met first of all by the basic difficulty of stating what is Anglican doctrine as such. Just as in the Protestant Church, where each theologian can put forward his subjective opinion in connexion with sacred scripture, without implicating thereby the doctrine of Protestantism, so too in Anglicanism important theological trends can diverge so radically that those outside may be left in doubt about the common doctrinal basis. Thus for instance, when a selection of texts from Anglican divines was published some years ago,[1]

[1] P. E. More and F. L. Cross, *Anglicanism, The Thought and Practice of the Church of England, Illustrated from the Religious Literature of the Seventeenth Century* (1951).

under the title of *Anglicanism*, it came under fire from its own ranks, because some theologians found it too "Catholic"[2] while others found that it was not "Catholic" enough. If, therefore, we are to present the Anglican doctrine of tradition, we must direct our efforts to finding some common feature in the variety of the individual pronouncements. With this in mind, we shall rely on the standing of the most important authors, being guided throughout by the foundation tenets of the Anglican Church, the Thirty-nine Articles.

The second difficulty arises from the nature of the subject. To find a place for it in the context of Anglican doctrine and theology is not easy, at least not in the way in which it can be normally inserted into Catholic theology. At the start there was no room for the doctrine of tradition in Anglicanism. It was suspected of introducing unauthorized legends[3] into the truths of revelation and hence of corrupting revelation by impositions and abuses. Yet in doctrinal matters, antiquity, the Fathers, and the primitive Church were held in high esteem and were quoted as arguments, even though from a special point of view only.[4] If then this investigation is to be pursued fruitfully, it will

[2] The word "Catholic", which can have five shades of meaning according to the *ODCC* (p. 251), means in Anglican theology mostly the common historical origin which is taken as the root of the great branches of the Church, the Anglican, Roman and Orthodox.

[3] Cf. Ch. Leslie, *Theological Works*, III, p. 32; Thomas Secker, *Sermons*, VI, p. 301.

[4] J. Jewel, *An Apology for the Church of England*, ed. by S. Isaac (1829), pp. 34, 37 f., 40 ff., 58.

be necessary to examine the faith of the Anglican Church as a whole and strive to see what is essential or only subordinate, what is normative or only interpretative, what is authoritative or only counselled.

1. *The problem of tradition according to the Anglican theologians of the 16th to the 18th century*

a) *The place of sacred scripture*

When we look in the Anglican Church for "the measure according to which we judge what matters we are to assent to, as revealed to us by God, and what not", John Tillotson gives us the answer: "that those books which we call the Holy Scriptures, are the means whereby the Christian doctrine has been brought" (*Works*, X, p. 239). They are not merely one means among others. As D. Waterland writes, "Scripture alone is our complete rule of faith and manners" (*Works*, VII, p. 3; cf. Paley, *Works*, II, p. 115; Secker, *Works*, IV, p. 295). It is from scripture that we can and do receive the fullness of revealed truth. Thus the sixth of the Thirty-nine Articles lays it down that "Holy Scripture containeth all things necessary to salvation, so that whatever is not read therein, nor may be proved thereby, is not to be required of any man, that it should be believed as an article of the Faith or be thought requisite or necessary to salvation. In the name of the Holy Scripture we do understand those canonical books of the Old and New Testament, of whose authority was never any doubt in the Church."[5] This was the position taken over and defended by the leading writers of the Anglican Church,[6] and so the word of God as contained in scripture became the sufficient rule of faith of the "Church of England".

One consequence of the doctrine of the sufficiency of scripture as thus laid down was the doctrine of the *necessaria*, that is, the truths necessary to be believed. As the scriptures received from the Apostles contain in full and sufficient measure the doctrine of salvation, they constitute "a rule both necessary and sufficient for men to be led and acted by in all their spiritual concerns".[7] Nothing outside scripture which claims to be a doctrine of faith is really necessary: it must be either contained in scripture or proved from scripture. Thomas Secker, in his *Lectures on the Catechism of the Church of England*, gives a simple proof of the doctrine of the *necessaria*: Christ possessed the Spirit without measure; the sacred writers shared in it, in so far as it was necessary for their task. Considering the end and object of the New Testament, it appears to be impossible that they could have omitted even *one* truth necessary to salvation.[8] Thus "the Scripture is put into our hands as the only sacred and infallible guide",[9] in the light of which we

[5] Quoted in the *Book of Common Prayer*.

[6] Cf. G. Bull, *Works*, II, p. 154; J. Taylor, *Works*, X, p. 384; R. Jenkins, *Reasonableness of Christianity*, II, p. 78.

[7] R. South, *Sermons*, III, p. 237.

[8] *Works*, I, pp. 71 f.; cf. W. Laud, *Conference with Fisher the Jesuit*, p. 113; H. Hammond, *Works*, I, p. 279; no proof is offered for Jesus's having willed to commit his doctrine to the New Testament only.

[9] J. Jortin, *Works*, IV, p. 373.

are to judge all doctrines. It seems in fact to contain all truths necessary to salvation, and the question of oral tradition appears therefore as superfluous from the very start.

We have not, however, yet done full justice to the Anglican divines on this point of doctrine. Anglican principles are not fully comprised under a viewpoint which is orientated exclusively on scripture. This is clear at once when we examine how the so-called "necessary truths of faith" stand exactly to scripture. All the *necessaria* are found in scripture, but not everything contained in scripture is necessary for salvation in the same way. "By fundamental truths are understood: (1) either such, without the belief of which we cannot be saved; or (2) such, the belief of which is sufficient to save".[10] The essential truths of revelation, which are given simply and directly, are called "fundamentals".[11] It is a postulate of Anglican theology that these important truths are clear and evident in scripture. The result is, according to Chillingworth, "that those places, which contain things necessary and where error was dangerous, need no infallible interpreter, because they are plain; and those that are obscure need none, because they contain not things necessary".[12] H. Hammond puts this affirmation in the form of an axiom which he claims to have taken from St John Chrysostom: πάντα 'αναγκαία δήλα, all necessary truths are evident.[13]

[10] R. South, *Sermons*, I, p. 51.

[11] D. Waterland, *A Discourse of Fundamentals*, VIII, p. 123.

[12] W. Chillingworth, *The Religion of Protestants*, p. 52. Cf. S. Horsley, *Works*, II, p. 107; J. Sharp, *Works*, VII, p. 75; J. Conybeare, *On Scripture Difficulties*, II, p. 102.

[13] "The Lord Falkland's Reply", in *Works*, II, p. 658.

9

It is important to observe the grounds on which the postulate of the "fundamentals" was based, since they are of no little importance in the struggles of the Oxford theologians of the nineteenth century, in which Newman also took part. The fundamentals have the function of rendering an infallible magisterium superfluous,[14] since both the learned and the unlearned can understand them.[15] They are a secondary postulate which follows from the primary, namely that there is one and only one source of faith which at least in essential points must be infallible and unmistakable.

A further problem which arises in this connexion is that of the interpretation of scripture. Even when the essential doctrines are unmistakable, "it cannot be denied", writes Sharp,[16] "that there are an abundance of passages both in the writing of the Old and New Testament, which are very hard to be understood". One Anglican writer gives a very light-hearted rule for dealing with such texts when he says: "The Jewish Rabbins in their comments on Scripture, so often as they met with hard and intricate texts, out of which they could not wrest themselves, were wont to shut up their discourse with this, *Elias cum venerit, solvet dubia*".[17]

Thus the reader and exegete need certain helps if they are to arrive at the true and fundamental meaning. One of the helps provided for interpreting scripture is human reason. John Hales admits, apropos of 2 Pet 1:20, that the

[14] F. Atterbury, *Sermons*, X, p. 274.

[15] J. Sharp, *Works*, VII, p. 76.

[16] *Ibid.*, p. 69.

[17] J. Hales, *Remains*, p. 28; cf. J. Conybeare, *op. cit.*, II, pp. 95 f.

10

Apostle says that "no Scripture is of private interpretation. There can therefore be but two certain infallible interpreters of Scripture; either itself, or the Holy Ghost the Author of it" (*Remains*, p. 21). But in saying this, he refers no doubt to the fundamentals, while for the rest, as F. Atterbury says, "every man may abound in his own sense and have his own opinions to himself; if he does but maintain these opinions with sobriety and modesty, without rending the unity, or disturbing the peace of the Church".[18] "All men have an inherent right to judge for themselves in matters of religion".[19] Though reason has often been a dangerous weapon in the interpretation of scripture, even in the Anglican Church, still, if used in the proper measure, it can be full of blessings: that at any rate is the mind of most Anglican writers. Thus J. Butler affirms that "reason is the only faculty we have wherewith to judge concerning anything, even revelation itself".[20] And Daniel Whitby maintains that in judging scripture "reason is regulated partly by principles of Faith, partly by Tradition, partly by Catholic maxims of her own".[21] It seems, therefore, to be general Anglican doctrine[22] that in explaining scripture reason is independent or at least can and ought to be invoked as an aid in the application of another means.

The means indicated here is undoubtedly the teaching of

[18] *Works*, II, p. 274; cf. p. 265.   [19] J. Jortin, *Works*, IV, p. 373.
[20] *Analogy*, II, ch. 3, p. 219; cf. Ch. Leslie, *Works*, III, p. 85.
[21] *Anglicanism*, p. 116.
[22] For the clearest statement on the subject, see J. Taylor, "A Discourse on the Liberty of Prophesying", in *Works*, VIII, pp. 98 ff.: "Of the Authority of Reason; and that it, proceeding upon best Grounds, is the best Judge".

the Fathers, the ancient Church. There are numerous testimonies of Anglican theologians which show that counsel is taken with the Fathers in the interpretation of scripture. "The Scripture interpreted by the primitive Church",[23] "as we find it interpreted by the holy Fathers and Doctors of the Church, as they had received it from those before them",[24] becomes the final court of appeal. D. Waterland declares that antiquity is sincerely treasured and highly esteemed by Anglicans in connexion with scripture,[25] and affirms as an absolutely necessary and inviolable rule that "that rule is Scripture, but taking Antiquity along with it, as the best comment upon it".[26] "Antiquity ought to attend as a handmaid to Scripture, to wait upon her; to keep off intruders from making too bold with her".[27]

When Waterland asks, in his *Second Defence of Some Queries*, "What harm is there in having recourse to the written tradition of the Fathers for the sense of the Scriptures?",[28] he implies that the Anglican view considers the teaching of the Fathers, antiquity, as a rule for interpreting scripture, as already part of tradition. We must now go on to consider tradition as something existing in its own right, and its function in the Anglican Church.

b) *Tradition as source of faith*

We should be inclined to think at once that tradition, in

[23] W. Laud, *A Conference*, p. 386.
[24] P. Gunning in *Anglicanism*, p. 91.
[25] "Importance of the Doctrine of Trinity", in *Works*, V, p. 255.
[26] *Works*, V, p. 429.   [27] *Ibid.*, V, p. 257.   [28] *Ibid.*, III, p. 468.

the theology of the Anglican Reformation, would receive the same treatment as at the hands of the Protestant Reformation and be considered as a source of corruption of doctrine. And in fact the supposition would not be false for some of the writers and for a certain type of tradition. Tradition was suspect, as having disfigured, overlaid and corrupted the "Verbum Dei purum".[29] This was the attitude of Bishop Gilbert Burnet of Salisbury when he wrote: "Yet as to matters of faith, we reject all oral tradition, as an incompetent means of conveying down doctrine to us".[30] In the same way, Hooker refuses "to add to the word of God" what he calls "uncertain traditions".[31] As "traditions of men", J. Milton holds that they should be completely proscribed, whether written or unwritten,[32] and J. Ussher likewise denies "that traditions of men should be obtruded unto us for articles of religion . . . or that any traditions should be accepted as parcels of God's word".[33]

However, these views do not represent the real attitude of Anglican authors with regard to tradition. There is a wide selection of theologians who speak in highly favourable terms of the genuine apostolic tradition.[34] We may begin with the fact that the existence of an oral tradition, which was not committed to writing by the Apostles, is admitted by Jeremy Taylor in his well-known book *Dissuasive from Popery*, when he writes: "Neither do

[29] Cf. J. Jewel, *Apologia Ecclesiae Anglicanae*, p. 117.
[30] In *The Exposition of the XXXIX Articles of the Church of England*, p. 93.
[31] *Works*, I, p. 420.   [32] *De Doctrina Christiana*, p. 357.
[33] *Answer to a Jesuit*, p. 32.
[34] Cf., for instance, J. Hey, *Lectures in Divinity*, II, p. 456.

13

we doubt but that there were many things spoken by Christ and his Apostles which were never written" (*Works*, X, p. 386). He even affirms that "if the Apostles had never written at all, we must have followed tradition, unless God had provided for us some better thing" (*ibid.*, XIII, p. 114). The argument is taken up and reinforced by Joseph Butler in his *Analogy of Religion*, as when he says, "Nay, we are not in any sort able to judge whether it were to have been expected that the revelation should have been committed to writing, or left to be handed down" (p. 222). Hence Chillingworth can even say: "I hope you do not imagine that we conceive any antipathy between God's word written and unwritten",[35] and W. Laud writes: "Some tradition, I deny not, is true and firm, and of great both authority and use in the Church, as being Apostolical".[36] Finally, we have the bishop of the great cathedral of Ely, Francis White, who makes the distinction between superstitious and unscriptural traditions and "genuine traditions agreeable to the Rule of Faith ... consonant with Holy Scripture", which come in unbroken continuity from apostolic times and have the unanimous testimony of antiquity behind them, and "are received and honoured by us".[37] These include the number, dignity, integrity and perfection of the canonical books of scripture, the interpretation of many texts, the Apostles' Creed, infant baptism, the perpetual virginity of Mary and the observance of Sunday.

The doctrine as expounded by Francis White undoubtedly comes very close to the Roman Catholic concept of

---

[35] *Religion of Protestants*, pp. 49 f.   [36] *A Conference*, p. 44.
[37] *A Treatise of the Sabbath Day*, pp. 97 f. (quoted in *Anglicanism*, p. 132).

tradition as source of revelation together with scripture. But here too we must clearly recognize that even White does not place tradition on an equal footing with scripture. He clearly subordinates tradition to scripture. It must be "agreeable to the Rule of Faith, subservient to piety, consonant with Holy Scripture".[38] We may take this to be the common doctrine of all Anglicans. Even Archbishop W. Laud, whom we have already quoted, maintains that anything that is to be eventually recognized as genuine apostolic tradition is merely there "for the better exposition of the Scripture".[39] It is instructive, "but not yet Fundamental in faith", in so far as it does not contain truths of scripture.[40] And Butler is convinced that if the transmission of revelation had been really oral, it would have been "corrupted by verbal tradition and at length sunk under it".[41]

We may best describe the doctrine of tradition in Anglican theology by saying that it is "necessary"[42] as the "guide to Scripture",[43] and the best commentary on it. Under no circumstances may it be considered as a source of revelation beside scripture and of equal value. Even if theoretically there had been a valid apostolic tradition in early times, equally valuable as a source, it would have no force at the present day: "We grant that oral tradition, in some circumstances, may be a sufficient way of conveying a doctrine; but with all we deny that such circumstances are now in being".[44]

[38] *Ibid.*   [39] *A Conference*, p. 53.   [40] *Ibid.*, p. 44.   [41] *Analogy*, p. 222
[42] D. Whitby, "Δὸς ποῦ στω" in *Anglicanism*, p. 116.
[43] H. Hammond, *Works*, II, p. 658.
[44] J. Tillotson, "Rule of Faith" in *Works*, X, p. 250.

c) *The significance of the Apostles' Creed*

It has already been noted that the Apostles' Creed is a
definite part of universal tradition. Since it has been handed
down without alteration or corruption to the Church of
the present day, its place in Anglican theology as source of
faith may be briefly examined. We read in Herbert
Thorndike that "whatsoever is said of the Rule of Faith
in the writings of the Fathers is to be understood of the
Creed".[45] It is the only tradition necessary to salvation: "I
say that only the Rule of Faith which is the law of attaining
everlasting life . . . is delivered by word of mouth".[46] Its
oral nature is also emphasized by R. Hooker, who affirms
that the Apostles handed it on, not to be written down on
paper and parchment, but to be retained in the heart.[47] In
spite of its being handed down only by word of mouth,
both its contents and its obligation are unquestionable.
Indeed, "all the points of the Apostles' Creed, as they are
expressed, are fundamental".[48] This may be proved in two
ways. First, it is a historical fact that the articles of faith
which are comprised in the Creed are "always the same in
all Churches and remain unchangeable".[49] "The assent of all
Churches" is enough "to assure us that any doctrine is true
or practice warrantable"—for which Tertullian's axiom is

[45] *An Epilogue to the Tragedy of the Church of England* (quoted in
Anglicanism, pp. 138 f.).
[46] "On the Principles of Christian Faith" in *Works*, II, p. 586.
[47] "Commentarius in Symbolum Apostolorum" in *Works*, p. 52.
[48] *A Conference*, p. 43.
[49] H. Thorndike, quoted in *Anglicanism*, p. 138.

16

quoted: *Quod apud multos unum invenitur, non est erratum, sed traditum*".[50] Then, as Waterland correctly recognizes, "as to the primitive Churches, their constant way was to enlarge their Creeds, in proportion to the growth of heresies".[51] A doctrine of development based on such a starting-point could not be content with the concept of the "unchangeable" Creed, which reflects in fact only one aspect of the formulas. To maintain the Anglican doctrine it was therefore important to note the second proof of the truth of the confessions of faith, sacred scripture. This was done for instance by John Pearson: "Whatsoever is delivered in the Creed, we therefore believe because it is contained in the Scriptures, and consequently must so believe it as it is contained here".[52] The Creed has, therefore, a special place in tradition, especially the Apostles' Creed, but it is not to be considered except in connexion with scripture, which is the guarantee behind it. Meanwhile no theologian was bold enough to give a clear and consistent statement on the true facts of the matter, as Newman did later, when he said that the Creed was "of the nature of a written document", possessing "an evidence of its Apostolical origin the same in kind with that admissible for the Scriptures".[53]

The Anglican view includes the liturgy, with its rites and

---

[50] I. Barrow, "An Exposition of the Creed" in *Works*, VI, pp. 394 f.

[51] "The Reasonableness of Retaining the Athanasian Creed" in *Works*, IV, p. 304.

[52] *An Exposition of the Creed*, p. 341. This text is all the more important, because Pearson was the greatest theologian of the Anglican Church in the seventeenth century (cf. *DNB*, XV, p. 615).

[53] *Via Media*, I, p. 249.

ceremonies, within the scope of apostolic tradition. It is part of tradition which must of course be distinguished from dogmatic tradition, since "the Church hath power to decree Rites or Ceremonies",[54] because they are "not of divine but of positive human right".[55] It is nonetheless true that all Churches have celebrated divine worship since apostolic times according to the traditional liturgies: "the way of serving God by liturgies has been all along the practice of all regular Churches since the times of the Apostles".[56] Hooker, following Whitaker, states that "those rites and customs (are) known to be Apostolical", but hastens to add that they have "the nature of things changeable".[57] Herbert Thorndike acknowledges that such rites have "the force of law, in directing the community of Christians in the public service of God",[58] but makes it clear that he considers the rites changeable according to different ages and countries, though in keeping with the mind of the Apostles.

John Durel examines the liturgical tradition from a completely different point of view. He goes beyond the formal elements to inspect the content, and considers how the liturgy provides a norm for Anglican theology. "It is a compound of texts of Scripture . . . of prayers, hymns, psalms, doxologies, lessons, creeds, and of thanksgivings".[59]

[54] Cf. Article XX of the Thirty-nine Articles.
[55] J. Ussher, *Answer to a Jesuit*, p. 32.
[56] Th. Comber, "History of Liturgies" in *Works*, V, p. 228.
[57] "Ecclesiastical Polity" in *Works*, I, pp. 304 f.
[58] *Of the Principles of Christian Truth*, II, p. 586.
[59] *The Liturgy of the Church of England* (quoted in *Anglicanism*, p. 179).

Thus he can say of the content of the *Book of Common Prayer*: "It is the marrow and substance of all that the piety and experience of the first five centuries of Christianity found most proper to edification".[60] It is not too much to say that Durel was a spiritual precursor of the liturgical views of the Oxford Movement.

d) *Church and infallibility*

"The Church is the multitude and number of those whom Almighty God severeth from the rest of the world by the work of his grace, and calleth to the participation of eternal happiness . . . it is named *ecclesia*, a multitude called out".

These are the terms in which Richard Field describes the nature of the Church.[61] He is depicting of course the whole, universal Church, which, according to his view, is embodied actually in different, separated Churches which are parts of the whole. This is the "Branch Theory" which is characteristic of Anglican ecclesiology.[62] The authority of each Church which is a branch of the tree is only partial, and they are all of equal standing. Rome, for instance, is "an elder sister",[63] and so is the Orthodox Church. The great house of the universal Church contains all: "Rome itself, as well as all other Particular Churches, dwells in this great Universal House".[64] The task of each

---

[60] *Ibid.*; cf. J. Taylor (quoted in *Anglicanism*, p. 174).

[61] *Of the Church*, I, p. 32.

[62] Cf. Newman, *Parochial Sermons*, III, p. 191; II, p. 674; *Mozley*, II, p. 111.

[63] *A Conference*, p. 312.   [64] *Ibid.*

19

particular Church, in its present rather truncated condition, is clear. It is to act as the Church of the present day and lead men to the one, decisive source of faith, scripture, which is not based on the authority of the Church but on its own intrinsic evidence: "But belief itself, that the Scripture is the Word of God, rests upon the Scripture".[65] In doing so, the Branch Church fulfils its essential function, which is to preserve the word of God in its purity and to hand it on without corruptions and additions. The particular Church is to some extent witness and guardian with regard to the revelation entrusted to it. But it is no more than that. Its declarations, expositions and official interpretations are not binding, unless they are guaranteed by scripture.

A certain hint of the authority of the universal Church is given by Anglican writers when they speak of the nature and importance of general councils.[66] But though all agree that a council represents the exercise of the supreme authority in the Church, their views differ very widely as to the extent of that authority. First, a general council is bound to give scriptural proofs for its decisions, and then, for all its authority, it remains a human court. As W. Warburton says: "The most specious exercise of human authority is doubtless in those Assemblies called General Councils. And yet . . . the same partialities mix themselves in their conclusions, which mislead civil Assemblies".[67] This fallibility is, however, denied by H. Hammond, who

[65] *Ibid.*, p. 84; cf. pp. 85, 89, 115 f. etc.
[66] *Ibid.*, p. 386; J. Bramhall, *Works*, p. 56 etc.
[67] *Works*, IX, p. 196.

maintains: "We do not believe that any General Councils, truly such, ever did, or shall err in any matter of faith".[68]

The revelation to which man commits himself wholly and without reserve must present itself firmly and infallibly. Thus this decisive question, on which men were divided, had to be discussed with special seriousness. But it is not easy here—in fact it is more difficult than elsewhere—to give an account of the views of the leading theologians on this problem. First we have the reaction of Anglicans to the claim of the Roman Church to infallibility. W. Laud finds the claim impossible, in view of the situation of Rome as a Branch Church: "For an infallible Church denotes a particular Church in that it is set in opposition to some other particular Church, that is not infallible".[69] For I. Barrow,[70] S. Horsley[71] and others,[72] the justification for rejecting the claim is to be found in the correct understanding of the Primacy text. "The promise to Peter", says Horsley, commenting on Mt 16:16–19, "consists of these two articles"—the power of the keys and the power of binding and loosing, which are personal to Peter. "The promise to the Church, which is next to be considered, consists likewise of two articles,—that it should be built upon a rock and that being so built, the gates of

[68] *Of Heresies*, p. 163.
[69] *A Conference*, pp. 4 f.
[70] "The Pope's Supremacy" in *Works*, VII, pp. 60–586. Barrow puts forward seven theses to refute the claim of the Catholic Church to infallibility.
[71] *Works*, I, pp. 285 ff.
[72] Cf. John Overall, *The Convocation Book of 1606*, p. 272.

hell should not prevail against it".[73] Hence according to this view, there is no office in the Church to which the power of infallible decision is attached. Consistently with this view, Archbishop T. Secker asks: "If the Church is to possess infallibility, what Part of it do you make the infallibility reside in?"[74] John Hales, finally, excludes all human claims: "For infallibility either in judgment or interpretation or whatsoever, is connected neither to the See of any bishop . . . nor to any created power whatsoever".[75] Voices like that of W. Payne are raised now and then to affirm: "It cannot be pretended that infallibility belongs to any but the true Church . . . she is an infallible guide or teacher",[76] and C. Leslie says: "Upon the whole I allow the Church to be the judge of faith, the only and supreme judge of it on earth".[77] But for Leslie, of course, this holds only for the non-fundamental truths; and in any case, these remain isolated opinions.

Nonetheless, Payne calls attention to the question of what Anglican theology meant by the infallibility of the Church. "That there will be always a Church infallible in fundamentals" is something that W. Chillingworth will "easily grant",[78] since it means only that "there shall always be a Church" to preserve and attest Christian

[73] *Works*, I, pp. 285 and 289.

[74] *Sermons*, XII, *Works*, VI, p. 311.

[75] *Remains*, p. 25.

[76] In *The Notes of the Church*, quoted in *Anglicanism*, p. 140.

[77] "On Private Judgment and Authority" in *Works*, I, p. 404.

[78] *Religion of Protestants*, quoted in *Anglicanism*, p. 113.

doctrine.[79] In this he also agrees with H. Hammond, who says: "but then this infalliblity must signify no more . . . than that Christ does and will so defend his Church, that there shall be for ever, till the end of the world, a Church Christian on the earth".[80] Laud likewise affirms: "I consider that all agree that the Church in general can never err from the faith necessary to salvation".[81]

Further enquiries imposed by the importance of the question, which involves some of the most basic issues, lead to the problem of where and in what subject the supposed infallibility is situated within the indefectible Church. The answer is—scripture. "In all questions, wherein religious morality is concerned, it becomes Christians, especially Protestants, to recur in the first place to that which they all acknowledge an infallible standard, and Protestants the only infallible standard, of truth and right, the Holy Scripture".[82] This is also the position of W. Laud, who speaks of "a most infallible certainty we have already in the Scripture",[83] and of Stillingfleet, who speaks of "the Infallibility of that doctrine, which is thereby conveyed to us".[84]

We are, therefore, justified in summing up the conclusions of our enquiries as follows: in the Anglican Church,

[79] *Ibid.*
[80] "A View of the Apology for the Infallibility of the Church of Rome" in *Works*, II, p. 569.
[81] *A Conference*, p. 240.
[82] George Campbell, *On Miracles*, p. 477.
[83] *A Conference*, p. 360; cf. p. 98.
[84] *A Rational Account* . . ., p. 193.

scripture is the first and last court of appeal, the one and infallible source of faith; any authority attributed to tradition beyond that of scripture—which is the decisive point—would be an immediate breach of the Anglican system.

2. Tradition in Anglican theology in the first half of the 19th century

The Anglican theologians who were contemporary to the Oxford movement deserve special attention with regard to their contribution to the problem of tradition.

It was the intention of the Tractarians to bring the Church of England back into the main stream of orthodox tradition and to restore its apostolic visage after it had threatened to degenerate into a Church controlled by the State. Hence it is only to be expected that the study of tradition would be one of the chief preoccupations of the movement, and that the doctrine of the Tractarians would provoke a reaction against such efforts on behalf of tradition. The theological literature of the time provides us with many testimonies to both suppositions.

We must begin by mentioning the name of Edward Hawkins. Though he was an opponent of the Oxford movement, he had laid down one of the principles which were to guide it, long before the movement was launched. As early as 1818, he had put forward a principle which was essentially a novelty in the Anglican theology of tradition. This was that "many of the most important articles of faith are rather implied than taught" in scripture, and that "universal tradition is our guide to Scripture".[85] The importance of Hawkins's influence on Newman, as of that of R.H. Froude and John Keble, will be apparent later.

Among the champions and defenders of apostolic tradition who now appear on the scene are Edward Churton, with his sermon on *The Church of England a Witness and Keeper of the Catholic Tradition* (1836), and Walter Farquhar Hook, whose *Five Sermons Preached before the University of Oxford* (1837) included one on the "Authority of the Church" and another "On Tradition". The most important contribution to ecclesiology, which, as has been noted, was the starting-point for the enquiries, was made by William Palmer. Palmer (1803–1885) was a graduate of Trinity College, Dublin, which he left in 1831 to become a Fellow of Worcester College, Oxford, where, incidentally, Francis Newman was then residing. He published his *Origines Liturgicae or Antiquities of the English Ritual* (two volumes) in 1832, which brought him into personal contact with Keble, Froude and Newman. He was also one of the founders of the "Association of Friends of the Church" which was later to support the Tractarians. His *Treatise on the Church of England, Designed Chiefly for the Use of Students in Theology* (2 vols., 1838) became immediately famous, and remained for half a century the great text-book for students and teachers of theology. In

---

[85] *A Dissertation upon the Use and Importance of Unauthoritative Tradition, as an Introduction to the Christian Doctrines; including a Sermon preached before the University of Oxford, May 31, 1818 upon 2 Thess 2:15* (1819), pp. 1, 17. Cf. H. Hammond, *Works*, II, p. 658.

1894 Gladstone could still say of it that it was "perhaps the most powerful and least assailable defence of the position of the Church of England from the 16th century".[86] Of particular interest for our subject are "The Notes of the Church" I, pp. 3–424, "On Scripture and Tradition" II, pp. 3–94, and "Authority of the Church" II, pp. 95–310. His discussion of tradition culminates in the following assertion: "I maintain, that Christianity cannot possibly admit that any doctrine established by universal tradition can be otherwise than divinely, infallibly, true" (II, pp. 47 f.). In other words, "we admit the necessity of both Scripture and Tradition to prove every article of faith" (II, p. 10). This attitude explains the response of Cardinal Wiseman, always anxious to be of service to the Oxford theologians, whose Lenten lectures of 1836 laid down the corresponding truth: "The Catholic system does not in the least exclude the Scriptures; . . . it holds that the foundation, or root, of all doctrines is to be virtually discovered in them".[87] Another who should not be forgotten is the court chaplain of Queen Victoria, Arthur Philip Perceval (1799–1853), who was also deeply concerned for the proper place of tradition within the Church. He had already written to Newman in 1835 to say that he fully agreed with Froude's opinion "of every bishop being absolute in his own diocese".[88] He found the opinion so

---

[86] Cf. *DNB*, XV, pp. 168 f.

[87] *Lectures on the Principal Doctrines and Practices of the Catholic Church delivered at St Mary's Moorfields during Lent 1836* (1836).

[88] *MS* B 11, 8 II, 97. Perceval is referring to Froude's letter to Newman of 30 July 1835. Cf. *MS* B 11, 8 II, 84: "Bishop Hickes, in his 'Constitu-

stimulating that he published in 1839 a book on the origin and character of the episcopal office, entitled *An Apology for the Doctrine of Apostolical Succession, with an Appendix of the English Orders* (1839).

The liturgy too received new life and contributed to the new reverence for dogmatic tradition. Palmer's *Treatise on the Church* had appealed to it: "the primitive Church practised many rites which are not contained in Scripture" (II, p. 67), but the main influence in this direction came from Edward Cardwell (1781–1861), a student of Church history who became professor of ancient history at Oxford in 1825, and succeeded Richard Whately as Master of St Alban's Hall. His historical writings threw new light on the Anglican liturgy, especially the *Book of Common Prayer*.[89] His work was to some extent along the lines of the Tractarians, who esteemed the Anglican prayer book very highly, and then took up the apostolic liturgy in particular, which they discussed in some ten of their *Tracts*. The *Tracts* were in fact the centre from which the notion of apostolic doctrine was disseminated. More than a third of the *Tracts* are devoted to the theme of the apostolic succession, and nineteen are concerned with the Church and Church history. To consider them in detail would take us too far afield; and we shall have occasion later to note

tion of the Christian Church' has convinced me, that in spirituals each Bishop was absolute in his own diocese, except so far as he may have bound himself by Ordination to his Primate".

[89] Cf. especially *The Two Books of Common Prayer* (1841) and *A History of the Conferences* ...; his collections of documents are listed in the bibliography, p. 196.

Newman's contribution. We may however quote at least one characteristic testimony, taken from *Tract* 24, "The Scripture View of the Apostolic Commission", which was composed by Benjamin Harrison. On the transmission of the apostolic ministry from St Paul to Timothy, the author writes: ". . . and now upon him was to devolve the solemn responsibility of being left in charge of the Apostle's testimony, and of handing it down to future ages".[90] Harrison here quotes the scriptural text which is so important for the notion of tradition: "Hold fast the form of sound words, which thou hast heard of me" (2 Tim 1:13, *A.V.*). It was in the atmosphere created by the *Tracts* that the other testimonies already quoted could come into being.

It will be readily understood that the view described above was not generally shared by the Anglican Church. The followers of the Protestant line in theology took up in particular a different standpoint, which we shall describe briefly.

In 1837 a short but sharp answer to Keble was published in Oxford under the title: *A Brief Examination of Professor Keble's Visitation Sermon entitled 'Primitive Tradition recognized in Holy Scripture'*. Its author was the prebendary of Winchester Cathedral, Dr William Wilson. In his anxiety (unjustified in this case) to uphold the purity of Anglican doctrine, he appeals to the absolute norm of scripture. The same tendency can be seen in Thomas Butt, of Christ Church College, Oxford, who followed shortly after with his

[90] *Tracts for the Times*, I, pp. 1–11.

Observations on Primitive Tradition and its Connexion with Evangelical Truth, with particular Reference and Examination of Professor Keble's Visitation Sermon, preached at Winchester September 27, 1836 (1837). We also have a reaction against the Tractarians in the book of George Holden (1783–1865), Rector of Maghull, whose *Authority of Tradition in Matters of Religion* was published in 1838. Holden is replying to nothing less than Newman's "Prophetical Office", and he states categorically: "While adhering to the written word of God, as the Rule of Faith, the Church of England does not admit any church, any traditionary doctrine, or any power on earth, to be the recognized judge of its true sense" (p. 167). The real judge, where difficulties arise, is reason: "The exercise of private judgment in religion is an unalienable right" (p. 140). In open contradiction to William Palmer (see p. 25 above) Holden affirms: "When the necessity of tradition is declared, it is at least inferentially declared that Scripture cannot be the touchstone of divine truth . . . which surely is the first step to the Romish dogma concerning Scripture and Tradition as a joint rule of faith" (p. 108). The result of his investigations is summed up curtly in his saying (pp. VI f.): "There is no evidence to prove the creed, or traditional doctrine of the primitive churches to be apostolical and divine".

Another sharp and uncompromising opponent of tradition is Philip N. Shuttleworth (1782–1842), fellow and tutor of New College, Oxford, Bishop of Chichester from 1840. His book, published in 1838, has the characteristic title: *Not Tradition, but Revelation*. The great Perrone quotes Shuttleworth as the typical representative of the *sola scriptura* principle, and uses his Anglican colleague W. Palmer to refute him.[91] Shuttleworth's whole book is not only consciously and deliberately directed against tradition and formulated in the strongest Protestant terms: it is also a manifestation of the opposition to the Oxford movement.[92] He is said to have denounced the Tractarians as "an active Popish party in Oxford".[93] Newman passed a devastating verdict on the work, not only because of its arguments, but also because of the tendentious style, which could include for instance this sort of description of Catholics: "Look at the Romanist attending the sacrifice of the mass. He kneels before the altar, an almost indifferent spectator, trusting that the mysterious ceremony of which he is an eye-witness . . . will some way or other operate to the redemption of his soul and the expiation of his sins" (p. 124). Newman's comment was: "Very superficial, retailing old objections, but specious and perhaps mischievous".[94]

This brings us to the end of our enquiries into the theology of Anglicans in the first three centuries after the Reformation, and gives us some indication of the dominant views at the time of the Oxford movement. We may now

---

[91] *Perrone*, III, p. 265, note 2: "Palmer eius collega in cit. Tractatu de ecclesia Vol. II part. III, cap. III negat ac vehementer negat principium reformationis fuisse, sola Biblia religionem esse protestantium. Nihil magis falsum est, ait ipse".

[92] Cf. *DNB*, XVIII, p. 176.

[93] Cf. Newman's letter to Froude, 22 June 1835 (*MS* B 11, 8 II 76).

[94] *Mozley*, II, p. 261; cf. p. 233.

try to summarize the doctrine of tradition in Anglican theology. It seems that the Anglican Church always accepted tradition as a help to interpreting scripture, though there was always a rigorous Protestant line which took its stand on the unadulterated principle of *sola scriptura*. As source of faith, however, tradition was always rejected, with various degrees of sharpness, and there are only a few theologians who form an exception to this rule. The Tractarians occupy a special place within the framework of Anglican theology, in so far as Catholicizing tendencies were pushed as far as possible among them. The collapse of their efforts is linked with the reaction of strong Protestant and liberal forces in the Church of England. This is the historical and theological background against which the figure of John Henry Newman stands out. A child of his times, sensitive to all its problems, he takes up the principles, tests them and chooses among them, and follows them consistently to their logical end.

PART TWO

The Historical Development of Newman's Views

1. *Newman's early acquaintance with scripture*

THAT THERE existed a revelation in which God had spoken of himself and of his relations to man, was one of Newman's earliest religious impressions and one which contributed decisively to his development. Even before he was capable of forming a personal judgment on the matter, he found himself confronted with revelation in the guise of sacred scripture.[1] The Bible dominated the

---

[1] Cf. *Apologia*, pp. 1 f.; *Mozley*, II, p. 401, note 1: "When in later years a young lady shortly to become his niece was introduced by H. W. M. to Cardinal Newman, he gave her at parting a golden ornament which had belonged to his grandmother, saying that to her he mainly owed his earliest love of the Bible". Cf. *Newman-Keble Correspondence*, p. 394.

religious atmosphere of his family, and it was the source of his first ideas of God. It was the image of a God calling and challenging, one who really spoke and acted.

This impression, which was of course at first to some extent an unconscious one, became clear and articulate when Newman found himself in contact with a man who felt himself personally carried away by his experience of God and who could tell him of this religious emotion. This was his teacher, Walter Mayers.[2] Newman received from him the impulse to reflect on the function of conscience, and to ask what it meant to be addressed by the voice which is heard in conscience, the primal organ of man's religious experience. It is characteristic that this impulse to reflection came to Newman to some extent *"cor ad cor"*, and that it evoked in him a personal, existential and whole-hearted response, which he himself called his "conversion".[3] It actually was a conversion in the two-fold sense of the word. There was a conscious turning away from the past towards God, who called him like an echo in his conscience. And there was also, indeed much more, "a return to an inner sense of the presence of God, and to an implicit trust in God's providence, which he remembered having had from his earliest childhood—indeed, which he thought was normal in children—but had lost for a while during a short lapse into rationalism at the age of fourteen".[4]

[2] *Apologia*, pp. 1 and 4.
[3] *Ibid.*, p. 5.
[4] Davis, *"Newman's Cause"*, p. 399; cf. Bouyer, *Newman*, pp. 32 ff.

In concrete terms this conversion meant that Newman had experienced the existence of his creator as an absolute certainty. As a result of this experience he felt himself from that day on to be unconditionally bound by the claims of God, and in particular to obedience. As this creator speaking in his conscience was for Newman identical with the God of revelation in the Bible, the principle of divine truth irrevocably laid down took possession of Newman's mind once and for all. Thus from his fifteenth year on dogmatic truth became the fundamental principle of his religion.[5]

Consciousness of being bound by the word of God became, during Newman's years at Oxford, an ever greater sense of reverent love for sacred scripture. One of his guiding principles in general was "knowledge is nothing compared with doing"[6] and he, therefore, began to study scripture more intensely and profoundly. He records in his diary that "I have generally . . . given the first hour of the day to reading the Bible".[7] Reading went hand in hand with memory work: "Last week or two I have been learning Scripture by heart, and have just finished the Epistle to the Ephesians".[8] "I have learned eight chapters of Isaiah by heart, from the 50th to 57th inclusive. May they be imprinted on my heart as well as on

---

[5] *Apologia*, p. 48.

[6] *Parochial Sermons*, I, p. 27.

[7] J. H. Newman, *Autobiographical Writings*, ed. by H. Tristram (1956), p. 187.

[8] *Ibid.*, p. 194.

my memory".[9] The basis of Newman's intimate knowledge of scripture as source of Christian faith and of his high regard for it as source of personal piety and consolation was laid in those years from 1822 on.

2. *The theologians of Oriel and the principle of tradition*

Newman was elected fellow of Oriel College, Oxford, on 12 April, 1822. For the young theologian this meeting with the leading lights of Oxford was to be of decisive importance, as the future was to show. Many years later he could still recall vividly and exactly how these theologians had contributed piece after piece to build up the great mosaic of his fundamental theological convictions or had at least set him on the track that he was to follow up.

It was for instance Richard Whately, later Anglican Archbishop of Dublin, who had first taught him to look on the Church as an independent community, instituted by God, and so not tributary to the State.[10] It was William James who explained to Newman during a walk the basic principle of the apostolic succession. And it was from Edward Hawkins that Newman received an introduction

[9] *Ibid.*, p. 195.

[10] *Autobiographical Writings*, p. 69; *Apologia*, p. 12. In *MS* A 17 Newman has marked sermons, pp. 90, 92, 146 etc., from his Anglican days, as "Whatelyan". W. Ward remarks in his biography that Newman also got the idea of tradition "as a guardian of religious truth" (I, p. 38) from Whately, but no proof is offered of the assertion. For the doctrine of the visible Church in Anglican theology, cf. J. Bramhall (quoted in *Via Media*, I, pp. xiii f.).

to the notion and the doctrine of tradition. Hawkins had preached a sermon in 1818 on the "Use and Importance of Unauthoritative Tradition", which Newman had heard as a student. But he had not grasped its importance, its originality and its implications, since he lacked at the time the necessary presuppositions. As a fellow of Oriel and now to some extent a colleague of Hawkins, he was given the sermon to read in its published form.[11] He studied it closely.

It starts out from the well-known text, "Therefore, brethren, stand fast, and hold the traditions which ye have been taught, whether by word, or by our espistle" (2 Thess 2:15, *A.V.*). Hawkins uses the form and structure of the New Testament writings, their unsystematic and to some extent allusive means of expressing themselves, to proceed to prove that scripture can never be fully intelligible without aid and guidance. Such aid and guidance exist in the form of tradition. Consequently, its existence is not due to the chances of history. It was foreseen by God and necessary. In other words, the usual and normal means for the transmission of the Christian faith is in fact oral tradition. But scripture then serves to indicate and prove the doctrines thus handed down.

Remembering the impression which these ideas made on him, Newman was later to say that they opened up to him a wide field of research.[12] We shall not be wrong in seeing in tradition the central theme of Newman's theolo-

[11] See Part I, p. 25, note 85.
[12] *Apologia*, p. 9.

gical effort, as the results of the following considerations should show more clearly. Hawkins's essay, which was in fact to be given a new presentation in later years,[13] was not the last impulse which Newman received during his time as fellow of Oriel. One of the basic features of Anglican theology is its effort to keep in touch with the Church Fathers of the first centuries. Newman came to learn this patristic principle from the classical theologians of the Anglican Church. From as early as 1823 he remained in uninterrupted contact with the works, theology and spirit of the Church of the Fathers.[14] In 1827 he began to study them in chronological order, which he later gave up for a systematic one.[15] He came to look on their times as the golden age of Christianity.

One concrete result of his studies was his book, *The Arians of the Fourth Century*, published in 1833. In this condensed and erudite essay he took the existence of tradition for granted in the Church of the Fathers. His only question was how it could be preserved from corruption in the course of time. And his final answer was that he found that tradition was given a fixed and unaltered expression in the Creeds of the Church.

[13] *An Inquiry into the Connected Uses of the Principal Means of Attaining Christian Truth, in Eight Sermons preached before the University of Oxford at the Bampton Lecture for the Year 1840* (1840).

[14] *Autobiographical Writings*, p. 72.

[15] Cf. his letter of 30 September 1842 to T. W. Allies: "Bishop Lloyd used to recommend beginning at the beginning—I found this in my case a failure" (*Newman-Keble Correspondence*, p. 197). Cf. *Lectures on Difficulties*, I, p. 372; *Newman-Keble Correspondence*, p. 196.

The sufficiency of scripture, as maintained in the sixth of the Thirty-nine Articles, caused Newman no difficulty as he put forward his views. Though he had enlarged the scope of Hawkins's principle in the course of his exposition, he still assigned to tradition a place which seemed inseparable from scripture. It is the authorized interpreter of scripture.[16]

Another doctrine of Newman's, found in its initial stages in the *Arians*, was to become of far-reaching importance. This was the function of lay-people in the general process of tradition. His ideas on this subject appear once more in his letters to his friend Richard H. Froude in 1835, where he affirms that "the maintenance of the faith is their clear prerogative" and raises the question of what power they may have in synods, judicially, and in legislation.[17] He develops his ideas further in his essay, "The Brothers' Controversy,"[18] and was to give them their final form in

---

[16] *Arians*, p. 55. Cf. *Church of the Fathers* (quoted in *Essays and Sketches*, III, p. 103), where the interpretation of scripture is said to come "from their received principles of interpretation or the traditionary practice of the Church".

[17] See *Mozley*, II, pp. 98, 100. On Newman's practical attitude towards the formation of the laity as a Catholic, see *Present Position of Catholics*; for his theory see "On Consulting the Faithful in Matters of Doctrine" in *The Rambler* (July 1859), pp. 198–230.

[18] "The Brothers' Controversy, being a Genuine Correspondence between a Clergyman of the Church of England and a Layman of Unitarian Opinion" in *British Critic* 39 (1836), pp. 169–99. Pp. 166–71 carry the heading "The Brothers' Controversy", pp. 172–99 "Apostolical Tradition".

the essay of 1859, "On Consulting the Faithful in Matters of Doctrine".[19]

Newman was to receive still further encouragement for his view of tradition. This time it came from a former fellow of Oriel, John Keble, to whom he owed some of his fundamental insights in theology.[20] Before preaching on tradition in Winchester Cathedral in 1836, Keble had sent him the text of the sermon for his verdict on it. Newman said of it: "What a magnificent sermon Keble's is. I think it is the boldest and most powerful composition we have yet put out".[21]

Keble starts from the text, 2 Tim 1:13 f., "Hold fast the form of sound words, which thou hast heard of me, in faith and in love which is in Christ Jesus. That good thing which was committed unto thee keep by the Holy Ghost which dwelleth in us" (A.V.). Keble then identifies "the form of sound words" with the "good thing", understanding thereby the whole doctrine of Jesus Christ, "committed" by St Paul to Timothy, a doctrine of which only some

[19] See note 17 above. Newman never reprinted the article except as an appendix in the later edition of the *Arians*. Cf. J. H. Newman, *On Consulting the Faithful in Matters of Doctrine*, ed. with an introduction by J. Coulson (1961).

[20] *Apologia*, pp. 18 f. Frederick Rogers wrote to Newman on 29 August 1836 that Keble "has been at a Visitation Sermon which he has just finished, on Tradition" (*Mozley*, II, p. 187). The Sermon was published in 1839 under the title: *Primitive Tradition Recognized in Holy Scripture; a Sermon Preached in the Cathedral Church of Winchester, at the Visitation of the Worshipful and Reverend William Dealtry, DD, Chancellor of the Diocese, Sept. 27, 1836*.

[21] *Mozley*, II, p. 192 (27 November 1836).

aspects can have been written down in the epistles. It is summed up in the Apostles' Creed, and is used for instance by Tertullian and St Irenaeus "parallel "to the scriptures. Keble draws the conclusion from all this, and affirms that in consequence the unwritten word of God, "if it can anyhow be authenticated, must necessarily demand the *same* reverence from us" as the written word.[22] Answering the question as to how such traditional doctrine can be ascertained in practice for the life of the Church of today, Keble says: "We answer by application of the well-known rule, *Quod semper, quod ubique, quod ab omnibus*".[23]

Keble's presentation of tradition undoubtedly constitutes the closest approximation to the Roman Catholic doctrine of tradition. Newman takes it the decisive step further in his *Essay on the Development of Christian Doctrine*, where he begins directly by criticizing the principle quoted from St Vincent of Lerins. In the light of present-day questions, it is perhaps not without interest to consider whether Keble had thought of two separate sources of faith in his exposition. And then the further question arises as to whether Newman's high praise for the sermon was also meant to embrace this aspect. The answer is not easy. On the one hand, one cannot suppose that Keble meant to abandon completely the fundamentals of Anglican doctrine. On the other hand, he was criticized as sharply as though he had

---

[22] *Primitive Tradition*, p. 26; cf. the formula of Trent, *pari pietatis affectu* (*Denzinger*, 783).

[23] *Primitive Tradition*, pp. 32 f.

done so.[24] That only one source of faith was envisaged may be deduced with sufficient certainty from a marginal note of Newman on Dr Wilson's criticism of Keble's sermon: "Fundamental mistake of Dr W(ilson) is thinking K(eble) w(ould) add essentials rather than insisting on a particular authority for them".[25] This means that "essentials" or "fundamentals", such as the faith derives from scripture according to Anglican doctrine and theology, are not added to in the concept of tradition upheld by Keble or Newman. They only receive a "particular authority". This view supposes that tradition contains nothing essentially new and that in its content it is at one with scripture.

3. *Newman and tradition during the Oxford Movement*

The object of the Oxford movement was to bring the Anglican Church to take notice of its proper independence with regard to external influences, to understand its proper mission in the light of its apostolic foundation. The members of the movement wished to link up with the Church of the Fathers in all questions of faith and morals, of liturgy and of the whole life of the Church. It was only

[24] There was a favourable review in the *British Critic* (July 1837), pp. 242–3: "The more this sermon is examined, the more its entire bearing on the present state of the Catholic Church in England will be seen". For the negative reactions, see the writings of T. Butt and W. Wilson referred to on pp. 28–29 above.

[25] Newman's copy of Wilson's pamphlet is filled with marginal notes, in which the quotation comes at the end.

in the Church of the Fathers that they thought the apostolic heritage was preserved, through the apostolic succession of the bishops. Newman's concept of tradition developed further in the context of these considerations.

In the years 1834 and 1835 we find Newman carrying on a controversy by letters with a Parisian priest, the Abbé Jean Nicolas Jager.[26] In the course of this correspondence, which had been begun by Benjamin Harrison and continued by Newman, the leader of the Oxford movement describes his concept of tradition under three aspects:

1) a tradition which interprets scripture,

2) a tradition independent of scripture (which can be justified by scripture, e.g. infant baptism etc.), and

3) a tradition concerned with discipline, ceremonies (customs) and historical facts.[27]

Newman contrasts these three aspects with what he conceives to be the further aspect admitted in Roman Catholic doctrine: "You, on the other hand, allowing our three uses of tradition, add a fourth, which we deny. You consider Tradition *per se* the sufficient authority for the

[26] In 1835 a book was published in Paris with the title: *Le Protestantisme aux prises avec la doctrine catholique*. It contains the correspondence between the editor, the Abbé Jager, and two Anglican clergymen, which had first been published in the *Univers* (*Jager*, p. 19) and then in book form. The Abbé's partners sign themselves B. H. and N, the former conducting the correspondence only up to 3 October 1834.

[27] *Jager*, p. 96.

Church's considering a doctrine fundamental".[28] The
formulations worked out by Newman in his discussion
with the Abbé Jager were used a year later, in 1836, when
Newman published the essay, "The Brothers' Controversy", which was mentioned above. It is the only work
of Newman's which deals specifically and exclusively with
tradition, and it was later given the new title of "Apostolical Tradition".[29] Newman's method again is to take
scripture as his starting-point, because it needs a reliable
interpreter: "the clearness of its teaching is not on a level
with its importance".[30] The antecedent probability of the
existence of such guarantees is confirmed by the history of
the Church. There is, for instance, an unbroken tradition
about the divinity of Jesus Christ, which offers a precise
commentary on the assertions of scripture. Another
confirmation is derived from the mode of teaching which

---

[28] *MS* D 6, 1, which goes on to quote Bellarmine: "Quia (Scriptura)
non est regula totalis sed partialis, inde illi accidit, ut non omnia
mensuret, et propterea aliquid sit de fide, quod in ipsa non continetur"
(*De Verbo Dei*, IV, 12, p. 205).

[29] This essay does not appear in the 1872 edition of the *Essays Critical*,
I, but it is in the new edition printed in 1897, which is quoted here. This
edition has the note that the "Letters of St Ignatius" have been transferred to the *Tracts Theological* and replaced by an article from the
British Critic ("Advertisement", p. IX). This can only be the article of
which we are speaking, which now appears with the title of "Apostolical Tradition" throughout (*Essays Critical*, I, pp. 102–38). It should be
noted that Newman made "large alterations . . . of a literary kind"
(*Essays Critical*, I, p. 137) for this edition.

[30] *Essays Critical*, I, p. 121.

is always customary in the Church: as Hawkins had argued, it hands on its message orally from generation to generation. Newman puts himself the decisive question, when he asks how this tradition is to be preserved without corruption. His answer is: "The safeguard against its corruption was the number and unanimity of its witnesses. The Canon of Scripture was another safeguard. Also it was kept in position, and from drifting, by the Creed: that is, by a fixed form of words".[31] This triple safeguard and guarantee preserved the apostolic tradition in the Church of the Fathers.

Newman grew more and more aware of the fact that the question of the transmission of Christian doctrine, in the Church of the Fathers and later in the universal Church, was not answered satisfactorily by the recognition of the Apostles' Creed as apostolic tradition. The more he sought to bring out its direct origin from the Apostles, its total freedom from additions, its even mechanical and sterile repetition down the centuries, the less could he convince himself that the process comprised and described the living testimony of the martyrs, the conciliar activity of the magisterium, the feverish enquiries and assurances of the theologians: in a word, the vibrant life of faith in the Church. The very fact that he continued his researches shows that he was not content with the results that they had given.

In the year 1835 Newman had been engaged, as we have seen, in a three-cornered discussion with his correspondents

---

[31] *Ibid.*, I, p. 126.

Richard Froude and the Abbé Jager,[32] in the course of which he arrived at a distinction which was to be important for his understanding of tradition.[33] It now appears in the essay "The Brothers' Controversy"[34] and becomes a major concern in his fundamental work, *Lectures on the Prophetical Office of the Church* (1837), in which he laid down the outlines for a special theology of the Anglican Church, the theology of the Via Media.

What is the distinction which Newman introduced? It affirms on the one hand that there are traditions which "passed from hand to hand, which were repeated and confessed at baptism, which were received and handed on from bishop to bishop".[35] They are "of the nature of a

[32] Tristram points out that Newman, stimulated by his differences with Froude (see correspondence of 1835) takes on the role of mediator in a fictitious dialogue between Jager, Froude and himself, and makes for the first time a distinction between tradition in the strict sense, i.e. apostolic or episcopal tradition, and prophetic tradition, which he defines as the voice of the body of the Church, the received system of the Church, the Spirit which pulsates in it. This may have been the birth of the distinction.

[33] Cf. Tristram, *Centenary Essays*, p. 215. In this connexion there is an interesting letter of B. Harrison, 4 August 1835 (*MS* B 11, 8 II, p. 90). Here Harrison calls attention to the description of Catholic tradition in Joseph de Voisin (d. 1685), *Pugio Fidei*. It is seen as a parallel to the Old Testament, and Harrison finds that it is a confirmation of the notion of prophetic tradition: "that the parallel holds so much the better with our line of 'prophetical tradition' from St John, and its several bends through priest, schools of the prophets etc., than with the time of the bishops of Rome."

[34] *Essays Critical*, I, pp. 130 f.

[35] *Via Media*, I, p. 249; cf. *Jager*, p. 375.

written document", equivalent to the Creed, and "an evidence of its Apostolical origin the same in kind with that admissible for the Scriptures".[36] They represent the content of episcopal tradition, which is anchored in the succession of the bishops.

But there is another type of tradition, handed on in other forms, which brings out better the dynamic nature of the faith as attested by the Church: interpreting and exhorting, searching and evolving, struggling and striving. Newman finds this form of tradition crystallised primarily in the liturgies, in the literature of controversy, in sermons and the like. He calls this living, fluctuating form of tradition the prophetic tradition.

Whereas the other form was like the hard, bony structure of the body, the second is like the flesh that clothes it. The former guarantees what is static and gives firmness and certainty; the latter guarantees what is dynamic and assures growth. The former is essentially unchanging and unadulterated, the latter is exposed to change and corruption.

Under these circumstances, one could say that Newman was trying to comprehend dialectically the complex phenomenon of the tradition of Christian doctrine. Thesis and antithesis enable him to grasp and depict its basic elements. But theoretically one can already affirm that the two contrasting theses cannot remain side by side, as it were in a sort of isolation, but that they call for synthesis. Only

---

[36] *Ibid.*; cf. *Letter*, II, p. 2, to J. N. Jager.

the corresponding synthesis can do justice to the reality of tradition and its way of manifesting itself.

4. *The breakthrough to the notion of development*

The assertion has been made that the notion of development appears suddenly in Newman's theology, without roots in what went before.[37] This might appear to be true: but only if one takes the University sermon of 2 February 1843 as the first expression of this idea, and only if one disregards the preparatory hints, the preliminary efforts to define the notion.

We might well consider Newman's early motto, "Growth is the only evidence of life" (*Apologia*, p. 4), as the first trace of the notion of development. The motto shows that he found the principle of dynamism congenial. He took it at first perhaps only as a principle of morals, a guide to his personal, spiritual life. But it was later to be mirrored in the history of Christian doctrines. A hint of this is given in a statement in a sermon "Steadfastness in

[37] O. Chadwick, *From Bossuet to Newman*, p.121: "The passage to the idea of development therefore looks like a leap, an intellectual venture to a doctrine which has no continuity nor connection with his earlier doctrine". Against this there is first of all Newman's own judgment, and there is no reason to doubt his uprightness and competence (cf. *Apologia*, pp. 194, 197; Chadwick, *op. cit.*, pp. 88, 123). The profound study of J. H. Walgrave in his *Développement* also tells against this view. Walgrave gives an enlightening psychological survey of the links between Newman's work and personality.

the Old-Paths" of 21 March 1830, which speaks of an "increase of light in the Church".[38] In the *Arians* he speaks more in detail of the definitions and new formulations which the Christological controversy gave rise to.[39] Looking back later at these remarks in the *Arians*, Newman considered them to be precursors of his doctrine of development.[40] A year later, in *Tract* 41, of 1834, he speaks of development as necessary in maintaining the purity of the faith: "Fresh and fresh articles of faith are necessary to secure the Church's purity . . . These articles were all hidden in the Church's bosom from the first and brought out in form according to the occasion".[41] When writing to the Abbé Jager in 1835, Newman justified the development of doctrine in the Church, as a right and a duty, by the need for adaptation to the changing times.[42] Here he also

[38] *Parochial Sermons*, VII, pp. 243–57. See the remarks in an unpublished sermon of 23 October 1825, where Newman says: "It is but an introduction to the Jewish system and intended merely to establish the fact, that there has been an increase of l(ight) in the Church, that there has been a progressive development of the gospel, that the Jews appear to have known more than the old Patriarchs and the Christians than the Jews" (*MS* A 17, no. 111, p. 3; cf. p. 1). These assertions are, however, confined to the Old Testament. Still, they may be taken as parallels and analogies, though hardly as a starting-point.

[39] Cf. *Arians*, pp. 36, 55, 59; *Essays and Sketches*, II, p. 288.

[40] *Apologia*, p. 197.

[41] *Via Media*, II, p. 32. Newman's comment on this as a Catholic was: "Here . . . the principle of doctrinal development is accepted as true and necessary for the Christian Church" (*ibid.*; cf. pp. 24 f., 32).

[42] *Jager*, p. 106: "L'Eglise doit limer et développer les fondamentaux, quoiqu'elle n'ait pas le droit d'en faire de nouveaux . . . L'oeuvre de l'Eglise existante". See preceding note.

indicates, to some extent *a priori*, the limits of possible development when he writes: "Development does not mean creation".[43] We meet the same theme a year later in the famous article "Home thoughts abroad", in which Newman indicates the limitations of the *aggiornamento* which were intrinsic to the Via Media: "It is only a substitution of infancy for manhood".[44] But here is the place to adduce the "prophetic tradition" spoken of above, which was used from 1835 on to describe and evaluate the dynamic or evolutionary element in the transmission of Christian doctrine. The *Lectures on the Prophetical Office of the Church*, of 1837, represent, as we have said, the climax of this line of thought. A year later, in 1838, *Tract* 85 appeared, on "Scripture and the Creed", without which, according to Newman's own statement, the *Essay on Development* cannot be properly understood. In this *Tract*, Newman makes use of the image of the seed and its growth, and compares the fundamental notions given in scripture ("seeds of thoughts") with what happens to the seed.[45] In the following year, 1839, appeared the essay

---

[43] *Ibid.*, p. 379: "développer n'est pas créer".

[44] Cf. "Home thoughts abroad" in *Discussions*, p. 18. Ambrose, the speaker of these words, may be considered as an Anglican of Catholic tendencies, who takes a critical view of the *Via Media*. M. Ward (p. 206, note 1) accepts the identification with R. H. Froude proposed by Christopher Dawson in his *Spirit of the Oxford Movement*, pp. 51 ff.

[45] *Tracts for the Times*, V, pp. 1–115; cf. O. Chadwick, *From Bossuet to Newman*, p. 129; *Discussions*, p. 174: "When a writer is deep, his half sentences, parentheses, clauses, nay his words, have a meaning in them . . . and admit of exposition".

"Prospects of the Anglican Church", where the same theme is taken up once more, and treated in terms of premisses which lead to conclusions, embryo and development, principles and consequences.[46] The great event of 1840 and 1841 was the famous *Tract* 90, which is basically only a consistent effort to bring the "developed" doctrine of the Council of Trent into harmony with the ideas of the Thirty-nine Articles.

After the failure of *Tract* 90, Newman gave his deliberate attention for the first time to the principle which had preoccupied him indirectly and incidentally for years—or rather, had pursued him. And perhaps it had pursued him because he had never been able to confront it face to face. It seems that from 1842 on, Newman, impelled by the need for continuity and consistency which was the bent of his own mind, and constrained by external circumstances, set himself to draw the conclusions from his actual premisses,[47] or where the conclusions were already taking shape, to consider them more closely, to justify, formulate and apply them.

The break-through to a new concept of the process of tradition came consciously and deliberately in the fifteenth sermon before Oxford University which has already been mentioned. Up to this, Newman had really envisaged only the mechanical concept of tradition which was generally in vogue. He had cherished the idea that formulas verbally indentical had been handed on, and that this repetition had

[46] *Essays Critical*, I, pp. 262–307.
[47] Cf. *Apologia*, p. 197.

assured the essential identity of the doctrine. In reality however, that is, in the historical reality of man, things were different. Here it was actually necessary that a system of ideas should change in order to remain the same.[48]

This new concept of tradition, in keeping with the organic nature of the spirit, represents a decisive turning-point not only in Newman's life, but in the theology of tradition. Its only parallel is in the teaching of the Tübingen school,[49] which is almost contemporary to it.

The starting-point for Newman's sermon is the text of Lk 2:19 and 2:51b, where Mary is said to have kept the mysteries of salvation in her heart, to meditate upon them. In this, according to Newman, Mary represents the prototype and model of the true Christian and of true Christianity. Christianity too, the true Church, has the duty of preserving well the revelation entrusted to it. The Church too will meditate upon it in the course of time. The result of the Church's meditation in the course of time on the word of God is displayed in constantly new insights. The exploring and explicitating thought of the Church is actually necessary, if it is to be true to the structure and content of the gospels[50]—an old theme of Newman, to

---

[48] *Essay on Development* (2nd ed.), p. 40.

[49] Cf. the comprehensive study of J. R. Geiselmann, *Die lebendige Überlieferung als Norm des christlichen Glaubens. Die apostolische Tradition in der Form der kirchlichen Verkündigung—das Formalprinzip des Katholizismus dargestellt im Geiste der Traditionslehre von Johann Ev. Kuhn*, in the series, *Die Überlieferung in der neueren Theologie*, vol. III (1959).

[50] This is true above all of the Gospel of St John; cf. *Fifteen Sermons*, XV, no. 7: "This is a phenomenon proper to the Gospel and a note of

which he now returns. The Church, however, does not proceed arbitrarily. It submits itself to the truth contained in scripture,[51] which thus becomes the starting-point for the expression of Church doctrine, in which are combined the enduring and dynamic qualities of tradition.

Thus Newman found in the process of development the key to the integration of the prophetic and episcopal tradition, and to their indissoluble connexion with scripture as the source of faith. He thus did justice to the historical reality of the Church, that is, to the changes constantly seen in creeds and dogmas. And he also gave due place to the human and dynamic aspect of the Church: the effort of thought and penetration, of formulation and re-formulation which the inadequacy of human words makes imperative. Finally, he also included in his new principle the divine and all-transcendent element of the Church: the work of the Paraclete, who alone preserves the truth of revelation and the revelation of the truth.

One of the most striking points of this sermon is the way it anticipates the concept of the Christian "idea". In the

divinity. Its half sentences, its overflowings of language, admit of development". Newman here refers to J. Butler, *Analogy*, II, p. 227, which had set him thinking along these lines. Butler writes: "And as it is owned the whole scheme of Scripture is not yet understood, so, if it ever comes to be understood before the restitution of all things (*Acts* 3:21), and without miraculous interposition, it must be in the same way as natural knowledge is come at: by the continuance and progress of learning and of liberty, and by particular persons attending to, comparing, and pursuing intimations scattered up and down it".

[51] *Fifteen Sermons*, XV, no. 7.

context, it becomes the integrating term for all Christian truths: "One thing alone has to be impressed on us by Scripture, the Catholic Idea, and in it they are all included".[52]

In view of all this, the *Essay on Development*, which Newman wrote in 1845 to satisfy himself, cannot primarily be concerned with expounding the doctrine of development. This was already clear in Newman's mind. What interested him was rather the existential question: where has the development of Christian doctrine been carried out truly and without corruption? Are there external criteria, which serve to test an unbroken line of development?

Newman chooses to begin with a critique of the classical rule of tradition as given by St Vincent of Lerins, who had laid it down in his *Commonitorium* that *quod ubique, quod semper, quod ab omnibus creditum est* is the way of recognizing the Catholic faith.[53] This principle, in spite of its widespread popularity, is basically too simple. It is not exact and scientific enough to provide the necessary proofs for the elements of Christian doctrine. What, for instance, is meant by *semper*? Does it suppose the explicit presence of a doctrine at any time under consideration, and hence always? If so, the doctrines concerning the Blessed Virgin Mary could not easily be shown to be the true doctrine of the Church of Jesus Christ, and in some cases it could not be shown at all. Or what is meant by *ubique*? Does it mean that every part of the Church has been penetrated by

[52] *Ibid.*, no. 28 (*Fifteen Sermons*, p. 336).
[53] Cf. II, p. 3; Migne, ed., *Patrologia Latina*, vol. L, p. 640.

a given doctrine? Or are qualified representatives enough? What sort should they be? How many of them would suffice?

The relative insufficiency of St Vincent's rule was, therefore, the occasion for Newman to seek for more objective characteristics of tradition, that is, of the true development of a system of ideas. And now he gives the seven criteria which were to become famous:

1. The Preservation of Type
2. The Continuity of Principle
3. The Power of Assimilation
4. Logical Sequence
5. Anticipation of the Future
6. Conservative Action upon the Past
7. Chronic Vigour.

In the light of these criteria, and with their help, Newman demonstrates that the Catholic Church of the first, third and fourth, fifth and sixth centuries, corresponds in type— or, we could also say, in structure—to the present Church of Rome. Or he can show that the power to adapt and assimilate, without detriment to the truth—a characteristic which puritanical and esoteric Christian circles have so often made a reproach—is a constant criterium of the Church of Jesus Christ. Incidentally, this very *aggiornamento* is once more playing a great part in the Church of Rome today. Or Newman shows that from the beginning the Catholic Church went through periods of flourishing and of wilting, of so-called triumph and of extreme peril. This recurrence of sterile and fruitful periods, with the unfailing forces of life flowing strongly underneath, also represents a characteristic which sustains the community of Jesus Christ and its doctrine.

The result of Newman's survey of the history of dogma in the Church's history as such was a fundamental and profound optimism with regard to the true doctrine and its preservation from corruption. It was the confirmation of the axiom put forward at the beginning: "If I have been arguing, in respect to the revealed doctrine, given us from above in Christianity, first, that in consequence of its intellectual character, and as passing through the minds of so many generations of men, and as applied by them to so many purposes, and as investigated so curiously as to its capabilities, implications, and bearings, it could not but grow and develop, as time went on, into a large theological system;—next, that, if development must be, then, whereas Revelation is a heavenly gift, He who gave it virtually has not given it, unless He has also secured it from perversion and corruption, in all such development as comes upon it by the necessity of its nature, or, in other words, that that intellectual action through successive generations, which is the organ of development, must, so far forth as it can claim to have been put in charge of the Revelation, be in its determinations infallible".[54]

At no stage of his life was Newman ever a purely speculative thinker. And his doctrine of development was not the result of theoretical considerations. It grew out of the existential stress of the believing and enquiring theo-

[54] *Essay on Development* (2nd ed.), p. 92.

logian. It led him to the Church of Rome, where alone he found living tradition in the sense of a development of doctrine, preserved to the present day.

5. *Newman and tradition after 1845*

Newman's decisive contribution to the doctrine of tradition is to be sought in the years before 1846. However, even as a Catholic, Newman was still concerned with tradition, in its static and dynamic aspects. His first piece of writing in this period, from 1847 on, served the purpose of summarizing his convictions on the subject in a number of Latin theses, which he put before the leading Roman theologian of the day, Giovanni Perrone, for his expert opinion.[55] In this treatise entitled *Utrum profecerit Ecclesia Catholica in cognitione sua fidei semel sibi ab Apostolis traditae?*[56] Newman designates the static element of tradition as

[55] Italian theologian (1794–1876), professor of dogmatic theology from 1824. His *Praelectiones Theologicae* (9 vols., 1835–42) were the most widely-used treatise in Catholic dogmatic theology in the nineteenth century. They treat of tradition or similar themes systematically in vol. I, *De vera religione*, where Perrone writes in the *pars posterior* (propositio II): "Sola proinde ecclesia est custos et interpres infallibilis divinae revelationis, sive viva voce per traditionem transmissae, sive litteris consignatae"; in vol. II *De Ecclesia*; vol. III, 2nd part, *De Verbo Dei Scripto et Tradito*. In 1847 he composed his famous *De Immaculato Beatae Mariae Virginis Conceptu* in preparation for the definition of the dogma.

[56] First published by T. Lynch, "Newman-Perrone Paper on Development" in *Gregorianum* 14 (1935), pp. 402–47.

verbum Dei objectivum, and the dynamic element as *verbum Dei subjectivum*. In the general exposition, the train of thought is more fluent and precise than in the first edition of the *Essay on Development*; but it is at the same time stiffer and less lively.

Newman finds that the word of God "is to be called objective, in so far as it has been translated, or will be translated, into dogmas, by Christ, by the Apostles, by the sovereign pontiff, by general councils".[57] It contains the deposit of faith of the Church of Jesus Christ. Newman calls the word of God "subjective" in so far as the faithful are preoccupied with it, in so far as the Church, under the guidance of the Holy Spirit, gains insight into this word and gives expression to its insight. Thence arises the process of growth and change and the new presentation of unchangeable truths already formulated. This process may be compared to the effort to penetrate a philosophy: in this case, to penetrate the "divine philosophy".[58]

Apart from a sermon on tradition, preached in 1849,[59] the later forties offer no further developments on tradition. And the fifties also passed without any essential declarations

[57] *Ibid.*, pp. 406 f.: "Obiectivum dicendum est, quatenus a Christo, ab Apostolis, a Summo Pontifice, a Conciliis Oecumenicis, in dogmata transierit et transiturum sit".

[58] *Ibid.*, p. 414: "est divina quaedam philosophia" (III, p. 2). Cf. *Callista*, pp. 327 f. : "Thus by degrees, Callista came to walk by a new philosophy".

[59] See appendix, no. 2.

from Newman with regard to the subject.[60] It was not till 1862 that Newman had the occasion of defining his final views on tradition. This was in the course of a letter which he wrote to Fr Joseph S. Flanagan, once a novice at the Oratory and now parish priest of Adare, Co. Limerick, who had asked for further explanations of points raised by Fr Ignatius Ryder in a controversy with W. G. Ward in the *Dublin Review*.[61] Newman's letter repays some close study, as it is one of his clearest statements on the theme.

The introductory considerations reveal impressively the great reverence which Newman had, not only for the revealed truth, but also for the personal freedom of the individual. He writes in this connexion: "I cannot bear tyrant majorities, and am tender about minorities; but I have no wish that minorities should kick up their heels and throw the majority into confusion".[62] Then, stating that he speaks "under correction",[63] he proceeds to expound his personal opinion on the problem of the development of the faith.

The deposit of faith is not "a list of articles that can be

[60] For a more general treatment of the topic, one could refer to the *Lectures on Difficulties*, where Newman discusses the "tradition" of the Anglican Church in the political sense (I, pp. 6, 7, 109, 193) and tradition in the Oxford movement. One might also mention in this period the *Present Position of Catholics*, where tradition in the broader sense is often discussed (pp. 51, 65, 67, 72 f., 85, 225 f., 236 etc.).

[61] *Gregorianum* 39 (1958), pp. 585–96 and *JTS*, new series, 9 (1958), pp. 324–35. See bibliography, "Sources".

[62] *Gregorianum*, *loc. cit.*, pp. 592 f.

[63] *Ibid.*, p. 595.

numbered",[64] and it is "not a number of formulae".[65] It is rather "a divine philosophy . . . a system of thought"[66] . . . "a large philosophy, all parts of which are connected together . . . so that he who really knows one part, may be said to know all, as *ex pede Herculem*".[67] This organic system was handed over to the Church by the Apostles, and is handed on from generation to generation in the Church. It was given to the Church in the concrete form of the Creed, for instance, and it came into "the mind of the Church"[68] along with the power of expounding it: "I believe the Creed (i.e. the deposit . . .) was delivered to the Church with the gift of knowing its true and full meaning".[69] Newman now asks how the "mind of the Church" is to be exactly envisaged. It cannot be the intellect of the Church, since "the Church is no person".[70] And it is not identical with the mind of the individual theologians and doctors, nor with the mind of the pope.[71] But it is active in the infallible decisions of the magisterium and makes use of the pope and the Fathers of a general council. "When the Pope sits in St Peter's chair, or when a council of Fathers and doctors is collected around him, it is capable of being presented to their minds with that fullness and exactness, under the operation of supernatural grace . . . with which it habitually, not occasionally resided in the minds of the Apostles".[72] Thus there is a clear and intelligible distinction between the Apostles, who

---

[64] *Ibid.*, p. 594.   [65] *Ibid.*, p. 595.   [66] *Ibid.*, p. 593.   [67] *Ibid.*, p. 594.
[68] *Ibid.*, p. 595. (Cf. "ecclesiae mentem" in *Perrone*, III, p. 326).
[69] *Ibid.*   [70] *Ibid.*   [71] *Ibid.*, p. 596.   [72] *Ibid.*

could always answer any question about the faith, and the Church. The Church possesses the faith in a global manner, and finds expression for it only partially and gradually, when granted and gaining insight: "I think I am right in saying that the tradition of the Apostles, committed to the whole Church *per modum unius*, manifests itself variously at various times".[73] Enlightenment comes to the Church "after the manner of an intuition or an instinct".[74] It also becomes apparent how Newman could hold that truths only implicitly contained in revelation were definable, even though they had not always been present explicitly as to their nature in the stream of tradition.[75]

The function of the "mind of the Church" also explains how the growth of doctrine in the Church is to be understood. Newman used an example from philosophy to illustrate the process. A good Aristotelian, for instance, could answer all questions in the same way that Aristotle himself would have answered them.[76] His mind, trained in Aristotelian thought, has developed a sort of instinct, and he also has the ability of thinking out problems on his own behalf.[77] But in the course of time, new problems are

---

[73] *Ibid.* Cf. "On Consulting the Faithful . . .", *loc. cit.*, p. 205.
[74] *Ibid.*
[75] Cf. *W. Ward*, I, p. 164: "His critics accused him of holding that the Church could define what was simply not in the tradition. His position was, of course, that what was might be at a given time denied, by those who did not yet master intellectually all the implications of this tradition".
[76] *Gregorianum, loc. cit.*, p. 593.
[77] *Ibid.*

constantly arising, and "technical" progress furnishes him with a more and more efficient vocabulary. Thus the follower of Aristotle will have a doctrine more comprehensive than that of his master, and he will actually know more than Aristotle did.

The common points and the differences when this example is applied to the "divine philosophy" are obvious. The "masters" of this philosophy are the inspired Apostles. In theory, they could have answered all the questions which the Church has answered in the course of time. They could even have answered immediately and directly, where the Church can only formulate answers at certain times and on certain occasions, according to the measure of divine guidance imparted to it. But *de facto* the Apostles neither knew the questions nor gave the answers. "The Apostle could answer questions at once . . . (but) the Church does in fact make answers that the Apostles did not make".[78] It is, therefore, correct to say that the Church of today does in fact know more than the Apostles did.

With this last comprehensive statement, Newman faced directly the essential problem of the development of doctrine in the Church. Even before the definition of infallibility, he had pointed out the necessary and intrinsic connexion between the transmission of the deposit, its explicitation in the course of time and the divinely guided, infallible magisterium. The final comment of his letter recalls his own experience of theological thinking: he compares it to tight-rope walking.[79] But it also lends his

[78] *Ibid.* Cf. *Essays Critical*, II, pp. 12–14.
[79] Cf. *W. Ward*, I, p. 125.

words the authority of convictions which he has gained in long years of thinking and testing: "I write this down with extreme caution, though it is the view which I have held for many years".[80] With these considerations, Newman gives definitive and detailed expression to his doctrine of scripture, tradition, the development of doctrine and the function of the magisterium.

In 1866, in his "Letter Addressed to the Rev. Edward B. Pusey, D.D., on the Occasion of his recent Eirenicon",[81] Newman had occasion to speak of the connexion between his Catholic notion of scripture and tradition and that of his Anglican colleague. As might have been expected, Newman simply offers here the converse of his argument from the *Essay on Development*.[82] He had then recognized, at the end of his years as an Anglican, that his previous notions on scripture and tradition were perfectly compatible with those of the Council of Trent.[83] And now, speaking as a Catholic to his Anglican colleague, he affirms that the difference between the two views is ultimately simply verbal. In 1878, when Newman published a second edition

[80] *Gregorianum, loc. cit.*, p. 596.
[81] *Lectures on Difficulties*, II, pp. 1–170. Cf. *The New Eve* (1952) in excerpts 1–66. Pusey had written an open letter to Keble in 1865: "The Church of England a Portion of Christ's One Holy Catholic Church, and a Means of Restoring Visible Unity, An Eirenicon". Here he expressed his opinion that union with Rome was prevented not so much by the doctrines of the Roman Catholic Church, as by the unofficial devotions (as for instance to Mary) and by popular ideas of purgatory and indulgences. Cf. *ODCC*, p. 1128.
[82] *Essay on Development* (2nd ed.), p. 339, note 1.
[83] *Ibid* (1st ed.), Ch. VI, sect. I, par. 1, note 2.

of the *Essay on Development* with some changes in the order, he again indicates that he has not altered his view of the two positions, as he propounded them to Pusey in 1866.[84]

The brief survey of Newman's views on tradition, which we have tried to provide here, shows clearly that the decisive insights, theories and advances were products of his Anglican period. It also shows that he did not give up the insights then acquired when he became a Catholic, and that he did not feel the need to give them up. As a Catholic, he only expressed himself occasionally on this important question. And his statements were then rather to supplement and clarify the position which he had arrived at in the eighteen-forties.

There are, however, some exceptions to this relatively homogeneous picture. The exceptions are practically all to be found in Newman's sermons. Thus in the outline of a sermon of 10 July 1849 and in another of 9 August 1874,[85] Newman seems to uphold the theory of two separate sources of faith. He writes in the first sketch that "the Bible is only part of the word of God", and in the second: "Hence we say that there are two parts of the word of God, written and unwritten". Such statements, and others of the same nature,[86] seem to contradict the clear and definite theory which he had worked out elsewhere. How are they

---

[84] See the note "Vid. Difficulties of Angl. vol. II, pp. 11, 12" in *Essay on Development* (2nd ed.), p. 339, note 1.

[85] See appendix, no. 2, 3 and 7.

[86] *Present Position of Catholics*, p. 317, Idea 72.

to be explained and what is their significance? It may first of all be said that Newman has left similar formulations from his Anglican days.[87] They are readily understandable, when one recalls that he had to over-emphasize the existence and necessity of tradition for the grasp of the Christian message, if he was to gain a hearing. The expressions were, therefore, formulated to some extent on polemical grounds. Similar statements from his Catholic days, such as have been instanced above, become understandable when one recognizes that Newman is here addressing an audience not composed of theologians. It was, therefore, pastoral motives that made Newman prefer the view then generally maintained to his own theological opinion. This is also true to some extent of the apologetical works which he wrote with readers of a different faith in view. With the help of this "rule", one can explain and justify all the statements which seem to depart from his personal theological views.

Some support for this explanation of Newman's procedure may be found in Newman's letter to Fr Flanagan, where he writes: "As to the Apologia, it must be recollected that it was not a didactic work—nor did it contain a statement of my own personal views about infallibility, but was addressed to Protestants in order to show them what it was that a Catholic fairly undertook in the way of theological profession, when he became a Catholic. I myself, for instance, have ever held as a matter of theolo-

[87] *Via Media*, I, p. 282; *Essays and Sketches*, I, p. 175; cf. J. Seynaeve. *Newman's Doctrine on Holy Scripture* . . ., pp. 44 f.

gical opinion the Infallibility of the Pope; but I carefully abstain from asserting it in the general view which I give of Catholic doctrine. I felt I should be as obviously wrong in setting down theological opinions, when I was declaring the Church's doctrine as such, as I have thought Archbishop Manning obviously wrong in introducing into his Pastorals the Pope's Infallibility; and I think I bore in mind, as I wrote, because I have ever remembered, our Bishop's remark, that what made Fr Faber's book on the Holy Eucharist so unsettling to nuns was that he mixed up dogma with theological opinion, and that in a popular work theological opinions ought to be kept under".[88]

The legacy which Newman left as the "loyal witness" to the tradition of revelation is given its best expression in a prayer where he asks for the gift of bearing witness in the truth, which we may quote to conclude our historical survey:

"Come ,O my dear Lord, and teach me in like manner. I need it not, and do not ask it, as far as this, that the word of truth which in the beginning was given to the Apostles by thee, has been handed down from age to age, and has already been taught to me, and thy infallible Church is the warrant of it. But I need thee to teach me day by day, according to each day's opportunities and needs. I need thee to give me that true divine instinct about revealed matters that, knowing one part, I may be able to anticipate or to approve of others. I need that understanding of the truths about thyself which may prepare me for all thy other

[88] *Gregorianum, loc. cit.,* p. 591.

truths—or at least may save me from conjecturing wrongly about them or commenting falsely upon them. I need the mind of the Spirit, which is the mind of the holy Fathers, and of the Church, by which I may not only say what they say on definite points, but think what they think; in all I need to be saved from an originality of thought, which is not true if it leads away from thee. Give me the gift of discriminating between true and false in all discourse of mine".[89]

[89] Cf. *W. Ward*, II, p. 365.

PART THREE

The Systematic Structure of Newman's Doctrine of Tradition

I. INTRODUCTION

IN THE historical part of this work, we tried to present the various phases through which Newman's thought passed as it changed and matured. His effort to penetrate the true nature of tradition had led him to go beyond the classical concept,[1] which confined tradition to a certain time and place. His study of Church history had led him to expand the notion of a static tradition. It was Newman's character-istic preoccupation with the divine providence which he knew to be always at work that pointed out to him the way

[1] Geiselmann in M. Schmaus, ed., *Die mündliche Überlieferung* (1957), pp. 184 ff., 188 ff.

which brought him to the true Church of the present day. This was the definitive phase, which is characterized by the extension and clarification of the doctrine on the basis of the teaching of the Church.

The object of the following systematic investigation is to bring out clearly Newman's definitive views. We begin with the doctrine of God's foreknowledge, which was the starting-point for Newman's whole doctrine on tradition. For from God's providence comes that mysterious enduring word, which is called revelation in its multiplicity.

II. THE "SACRAMENTAL" WORD

1. *The going forth from God*

THE WORD which is chosen to be the bearer of the truth of divine revelation goes forth from God. Like everything divine, it is fraught with unfathomable depths of mystery.[1] But it is embodied in human modes of speech and expression, and so becomes intelligible to man. It appears, so to speak, in the shell of an external form, within which its content is concealed.[2] Its content is heavenly truth, a mystery, a sacrament.[3] Thus the word of revelation to Newman's mind was a canal through which supernatural grace and knowledge of things eternal could flow to man.[4]

---

[1] *Jager*, p. 336: "chaque mot de la révélation divine a un sens profond".
[2] *Ibid.*: "Il est l'enveloppe extérieure d'une vérité céleste".
[3] *Ibid.*: "un mystère ou un sacrement". Cf. *Via Media*, I, pp. 292 f.
[4] *Stray Essays*, I, par. 18.

It follows that the divine word works in a way like that of the sacraments. It rids men of the darkness of ignorance[5] and bestows the light of truth.[6] It goes forth from God and does not return to him empty, according to the well-known text of Isaiah, which Newman quotes in this connexion.[7] It fulfils the work for which it is sent. It is, therefore, unconquerable. Still, it does not coerce man. On the contrary, it addresses him in his freedom, inviting him to open his heart to the divine summons. But since it is clothed in human guise, man can close his heart and stop it entering.[8]

In its essential constitution as well as in all its expressions the word of revelation, according to Newman, possesses a quasi-sacramental character. This principle of Newman's is not to be understood in the developed sense of the modern "theology of the word",[9] but his assertions point in this direction. This fundamental concept dominates all Newman's thought on the subject and finds expression in his notion of the divine word in tradition and of its acting upon man in its encounter with him.

[5] *MS* A 16, 4 I, p. 169: "Why has God given us a 'Word'? Because we are so ignorant".

[6] Cf. *Meditations*, p. 210.

[7] Is 55:11; cf. *Parochial Sermons*, VI, p. 271; *Newman-Keble Correspondence*, p. 186.

[8] *Ibid.*: "Nothing can stop it but a closed heart".

[9] Cf. K. Rahner, *Schriften zur Theologie* (3rd ed., 1958), I, pp. 29 f., English translation: *Theological Investigations* (1961), I; H. Schlier, *Wort Gottes* (1958); J. Betz, "Wort und Sakrament" in *Verkündigung und Glaube, Festgabe für F.X. Arnold* (1958), pp. 76–99 (with literature).

2. *Divine providence*

God's universal plan for the world, which he unfolds and puts into effect in time, is characterized by the fact that "God does nothing without some wise and good reason".[10] As we contemplate God's action, we see that "the world goes on by fixed laws",[11] as is shown by the laws of general and particular providence.[12] At the same time man seems to be able to recognize certain breaches of these laws,[13] which again appear in ordered and regular form. This simply proves the existence of a second set of valid laws: "There are two providential systems in operation among us, the visible and the invisible, intersecting as it were each other, and having a certain territory in common".[14] Here, where the two planes of the natural and supernatural intersect, divine revelation takes place, and "Revelation so melts into Providence that we cannot draw the line between them".[15] Thus it is understandable that divine providence, which manifests itself in general in the laws of nature, and in particular in God's "guiding hand" which cares for man,[16] should be especially evident in bringing about revelation. In other words: the marvellous and purposeful development of tradition which is seen in

[10] *Parochial Sermons*, I, p. 328.

[11] *Sermon Notes*, p. 380.

[12] *Ibid.*, p. 380; cf. *Parochial Sermons*, III, pp. 114 f.; V, p. 84.

[13] i.e. miracle.

[14] *Miracles*, pp. 186 f.

[15] *Via Media*, I, p. 92.

[16] *Parochial Sermons*, V, p. 84; cf. III, pp. 123, 126; II, pp. 98 f.

the history of revelation,[17] allows of no other conclusion than that here the general principle of divine providence receives confirmation. Thus the providential action of God is the beginning and the end: from it stem revelation and tradition in general, and oral tradition in particular; from it they derive their life and force.

Newman argued, in his *Essay on Development*, from the nature of revelation and the necessity of development to the existence of a divine protection of development: "If development must be, then, whereas Revelation is a heavenly gift, He who gave it virtually has not given it, unless He has also secured it from perversion and corruption, in all such developments as come upon it by the necessity of its nature".[18] Here God's "overruling" providence is at work,[19] a "Providence never wanting to His Church".[20] It preserves incorrupt the truth once given, because "Providence does nothing in vain",[21] that "wonderful Providence which is so silent, yet so efficacious".[22] "The more secret God's hand is, the more powerful, the more silent, the more awful" is the working of Providence.[23] From the world, "God hides his Provi-

---

[17] Cf. *Lectures on Difficulties*, II, pp. 244 f.

[18] *Essay on Development* (2nd ed.), p. 92.

[19] *Grammar of Assent*, p. 351; *Parochial Sermons*, VII, p. 64; *Essays Critical*, II, p. 90 etc.

[20] *Lectures on Difficulties*, II, pp. 306 f.

[21] *Ibid.*, I, p. 98.

[22] *Parochial Sermons*, IV, p. 259.

[23] *Ibid.*, p. 265.

dence, yet carries it forward" to its appointed end.[24] Thus we meet once more the doctrine of the two planes of God's action, which is so characteristic of Newman, when he writes: "the visible world is the instrument, yet the veil, of the world invisible".[25] At this decisive point, the basic notion of analogy, which Newman had derived from Butler,[26] is applied to the truths of revelation: "The God who wrought them by human means in their first introduction, still preserves them by the same".[27] Here is disclosed, according to Newman, the central element of the divine plan for the world. This centre is the Incarnation,[28] where the union of the divine and human is realized in the person of Jesus Christ.

From this source flow the streams from which tradition is fed. God who gives revelation also preserves and protects it: God who teaches man also guides and directs him infallibly. We are at the source from which tradition flows. We can see the loftiness of its origin, and recognize that there is nothing higher. It follows at once that nothing could or ever can hold up its course. But it also follows

[24] *Ibid.*, II, p. 114.

[25] *Essays Critical*, II, p. 192; on the term "veil" see *Parochial Sermons*, V, p. 10 etc. and cf. the use of "shadow" in *Parochial Sermons*, V, p. 4; I, pp. 20 f.; VII, pp. 96 f.; VI, pp. 98 f. and often.

[26] Cf. *Apologia*, p. 19. Butler's *Analogy* (see bibliography) was first published in 1736. Cf. K. Dick, *Das Prinzip der Analogie nach Butler and Newman.* Unprinted dissertation, Munich (1958).

[27] *Parochial Sermons*, VII, p. 236.

[28] Cf. *Essay on Development* (2nd ed.), pp. 325 f.

that the mysterious water of this spring demands to be constantly and intensively sounded.[29]

3. *The work of the Holy Spirit*

As divine providence preserves and guides creation in general and particular, it is the third person of the Trinity who is the immediate source of life in the community of the New Covenant. "The dispensation of the Son visible

---

[29] In his article, "Newman et le développement dogmatique" in the *Revue des Sciences Religieuses* 32 (1958), pp. 197–213, M. Nédoncelle investigates the origin of the metaphor of the source and the stream (cf. *Essay on Development*, 2nd ed., p. 40: "Indeed it is sometimes said that the stream is clearest near the spring. Whatever use may be made of this image, it does not apply to the history of a philosophy or sect, which, on the contrary, is more equable, and purer and stronger when its bed has become deep and broad and full"). He comes to the conclusion that the comparison is an allusion to a passage in Edward Burton's *Testimonies of the Ante-Nicene Fathers to the Divinity of Christ* (1826). Burton writes: "It is an evident truth that all corruptions have a gradual growth; and it is equally clear and irrefutable, that doctrines have all the greater chance to be pure and original, the nearer they are to their enunciation; just as we are more likely to find a stream clear and pure, the closer we come to the spring" (*ibid.*, 2nd ed., 1829, p. III). Nédoncelle thinks that the two scholars probably debated their views (*op. cit.*, p. 211) or that this is at least suggested by a polemical utterance of Burton in the 6th edition of his *History of the Christian Church from the Ascension of Jesus Christ to the Conversion of Constantine* (1845), where he writes: "To assert that Christianity has been perfected as the world has become more enlightened, cannot be the work of a man who has really understood what the Gospel is".

upon e arth was transient, the dispensation of the Holy Spirit invisibly dwelling in his stead is perpetual".[30] Having come into the world to teach and redeem mankind, as the Logos who proceeds eternally from the Father,[31] he returned from the world to the Father. The Holy Spirit now guides the Church, "until the second coming of the Son of God".[32]

"It is a general law of divine providence" that the Holy Spirit should give glory to the Son of God in a special way:[33] "He was sent from Christ to glorify and illuminate the words of Christ".[34] His work is not merely the continuation of Christ's work: it is in a way identical with it: "The Ghost's coming is so really His (Christ's) coming, that we might as well say that He was not here in the days of His flesh, . . . as deny that He is here now, when He is here by His divine spirit".[35] And it is the completion of the work of the Incarnation. Before the coming of the Spirit, the believers were like the dry bones in the vision of the prophet. Now they have become the organs of the divine spirit which animates all.[36] Once, all that existed was the personal connexion between the God-fearing, which was

[30] *Office*, p. 4.
[31] Cf. *Tracts Theological*, p. 238.
[32] *Office*, p. 1.
[33] *Parochial Sermons*, IV, p. 254.
[34]*Ibid.*, III, p. 73.
[35]*Ibid.*,IV, pp. 248 f.; cf. IV, p; 169 and J. A. Möhler, *Die Einheit in der Kirche*, ed. by J. R. Geiselmann (1957), which uses the same principles of pneumatology (pp. 5 ff., 9, 22, 25, 248 etc.).
[36] Cf. *Parochial Sermons*, IV, pp. 170 f.

menaced, brittle and capable of dissolution. But now there exists a mysterious organism, a mystical body, indissolubly united with God in the Holy Spirit.[37]

This body is the Church, the great achievement through which the Spirit works: "That, I say, is the first great work and the foundation of all the works of the Holy Ghost".[38] Pentecost was the turning-point: "All that we have of good comes from this day",[39] the day when "the lifegiving Spirit" manifested the Church visibly before the world.[40] All graces are imparted to men by this channel, and the Spirit in the Church guarantees for all time both the unity of faith and the message of truth.[41]

The divine authority of the truth, which makes its imperious summons heard through the Church, is guaranteed by the work of the Holy Spirit, the "guide and teacher of the faithful".[42] He is "the Blessed Spirit promised to us as a second teacher of truth",[43] who first "inspired the Holy Evangelists to record the life of Christ and directed them" and "next . . . commented upon these, and unfolded their meaning in the Apostolic Epistles".[44] "The Paraclete" remains "the Life of the Church" throughout the centuries,[45] leading the Church, as Christ had promised, to all

[37] Cf. *Office*, p. 11.
[38] *MS* transcription A 29, 5, p. 2 (27 August 1876).
[39] *MS* A 16, 4 I, p. 51.   [40]*Ibid.*, p. 42.
[41] Cf. *Office*, p. 9.
[42] *Ibid.*, p. 4, cf. p. 6.
[43] *Fifteen Sermons*, p. 83.
[44] *Parochial Sermons*, II, p. 227.
[45] *Meditations*, pp. 311–13.

truth, which is, therefore, "a subject matter much more diversified than that on which our Lord had revealed Himself before Him".[46]

But the teaching office of the Holy Spirit goes much further and deeper. Wherever revelation has taken root, in scripture or tradition, in the faithful or in the magisterium, it is he alone who gives knowledge of the truth, and hence no true progress in the understanding of revelation ever takes place without his assistance and enlightenment.[47] As Christ had promised, the Spirit "will explain that which was given";[48] by his help, the truths brought by Christ are handed on and collected and made understandable.[49] The Spirit, therefore, brings no new revelation, since Christ gave the full and hence the final revelation to his Apostles, but he guides the Church as its understanding of these truths grows ever clearer.[50]

It has already been noted that creation continues to need the sustaining hand of God.[51] So too the truth once revealed needs to be protected and upheld against corruption and perversion, and this is the work of the Spirit of truth. His activities are different, according to whether they bear on sacred scripture or on the unwritten words of Jesus.[52] But he who preserves and interprets the scripture by his illumination is also the preserver of tradition, and his work goes on until the end of time. Thus one can rightly say with Newman that "the office of the Holy Ghost as the

[46] *Fifteen Sermons*, p. 83.
[47] Cf. *Office*, p. 6 and *MS* C 5, 1, appendix, no. 6.
[48] *MS* C 5, 1.   [49] *Ibid.*   [50] *Ibid.*
[51] See pp. 72–75 above.   [52] Cf. *MS* C 5, 1.

guide and teacher of the faithful, is as full and perfect in all its power and prerogatives at this hour, as it was on the day of Pentecost",[53] and that it will remain so beyond the present day until the consummation of the world.[54]

We can know well enough, by reflecting on our natural and supernatural knowledge, how the Spirit of God works.[55] His intervention is for the most part organic and at first imperceptible. Like the work of providence, "His operation has been calm, equable, gradual, far-spreading, overtaking, intimate, irresistible".[56] He is "the inward light"[57] and "a source of life",[58] "a source of life amid the chaos".[59] Without him we cannot survive in grace: "we are indeed constantly and unceasingly dependent on the Holy Ghost for our heavenly life, as we are on the air around for our natural life".[60] And without his impulse, neither we nor the world can reach the great goal: "By his wonder-working grace all things tend to perfection".[61]

Sanctification, "the highest excellence to which we ordinarily attain",[62] is the ultimate object of the Spirit's light-giving and life-giving work. "What He is towards angels, towards glorified Saints as Moses and Elias . . . towards the Jews, towards the Heathen, towards the Christian militant, what he is in the Church, in the

[53] *Office*, p. 4. [54] Cf. *Office*, pp. 4 f. [55] See notes 21–23 above.
[56] *Subjects of the Day*, p. 128.
[57] *Parochial Sermons*, II, p. 218, cf. VIII, p. 152.
[58] *Ibid.*, II, p. 218, cf. IV, p. 173.
[59] *Ibid.*, II, p. 218.
[60] *MS* A 17, no. 5, p. 1.
[61] *Parochial Sermons*, II, p. 228. [62] *Ibid.*, I, p. 147.

individual, in the Apostle, in the Prophet, in the Apocryphal writer, in the Doctor and Teacher, is all holy, but admits of kind and of degree".[63]

III. THE WORD IN THE WORLD

1. *The heathens*

MAN's relationship to God was never confined to the intimations of conscience, to the affirmations of reason, to the "traces of his presence" in creation.[1] Though not a "traditionalist" in the sense that he denied the powers of reason, Newman could say: "It is very doubtful, whether the phenomena of the visible world would in themselves have brought us to a knowledge of the Creator; but the universal tradition of His existence has been from the beginning His own comment upon them, graciously preceding the study of the evidence".[2] It is probably

[63] *Via Media*, II, p. 172.

[1] *Discourses*, p. 278.

[2] *Arians*, p. 152. W. Ward has already emphasized that such assertions of Newman are no ground for taking him to be a traditionalist in the sense in which the term was condemned, *Denzinger*, 1649–52 (I, p. 43). And in fact Newman never doubted the independent validity of reason, or asserted the necessity of tradition as absolute in the attainment of truth (cf. *Parochial Sermons*, VIII, p. 96). H. F. Davis comments, in *Blackfriars* (July 1958), p. 316: "Newman's fundamental belief in reason is shown by the fact that he made logical sequence a test of faithful developments". Along with these important principles, however, Newman did not lose sight of the intellectualism which was so

impossible to point to any people where there was no tradition of religious truths.[3] Thus the tradition of revealed truth is as universal as revelation itself,[4] and just as ancient. Tradition begins with revelation, that is, with the first "paradisiacal illumination" from which sprang the "endemic traditions"[5] which Newman calls the "Dispensation of Paganism".[6] "From the beginning the Moral Governor of the world has scattered the seeds of truth far and wide over its extent".[7] Penetrating all parts of the world, the divine truths have been accepted and turned to account and handed on in all lands, "without their population knowing whence these truths came".[8]

The form of religion which results from superstition, "nature's best offering . . . in the presence of a holy and offended God"[9] when combined with a traditional but partial and distorted revelation, is given the name of "Natural Religion".[10] But it is not a merely natural thing: "The religion of Nature . . . has been a tradition or an

much a product of his day and which the traditionalist doctrines aimed at overcoming. His own contribution was the pre-eminent place he gave to the traditional nature of the divine revelation. "It was an appeal to the wisdom of the ages against the intellectualism of the hour" (*W. Ward*, I, p. 44).

[3] *Fifteen Sermons*, II, p. 18.

[4] *Arians*, p. 80.

[5] *Grammar of Assent*, p. 408.

[6] *Arians*, p. 81.

[7] *Essays Critical*, II, p. 231. Cf. *Arians*, p. 86, "the scattered fragments"

[8] *Grammar of Assent*, p. 386.

[9] *Fifteen Sermons*, VI, p. 118; cf. *Via Media*, I, p. lxix.

[10] *Grammar of Assent*, pp. 389–408.

interposition vouchsafed to a people from above".[11] Thus "*Spiritus Domini replevit orbem terrarum*. Grace is given for the merits of Christ all over the earth".[12]

The means whereby the God-fearing pagan is rendered capable of a religious life and of accepting the religious truths which are handed down to him is conscience or reason. He must let himself be led by the "inward sense"[13] of conscience and the reasoning power of thought alone, under the guidance of divine providence.

Newman also indicates some of the permanent and fundamental truths thus handed down: "Nor again are we to suppose that there were not constant traditions flying through the nations concerning the existence of one supreme maker and governor of the world, of his greatness and wisdom and knowledge and benevolence to man".[14] Along with the doctrines held in common by the pagans on many subjects, Newman can also enumerate common traditional customs or rites in the various cultic communities. These include genuflections, prescribed clothing, silence and taking off the shoes.[15] He also notes common basic rules like assemblies for worship, organized corporations with laws and officials, feast-days, churches etc.[16] Since such common customs, laws and truths are found in different peoples, each possessing their own line of

[11] *Ibid.*, p. 404.
[12] *Lectures on Difficulties*, I, p. 83.
[13] *Parochial Sermons*, II, p. 18.
[14] *MS* A 17, no. 110, p. 2.
[15] *Parochial Sermons*, VIII, p. 5.
[16] Cf. *Ibid.*, V, pp. 171–5.

tradition, the uniformity evidently confirms the unity of origin postulated at the beginning for all religious traditions: they all derive from the tradition of the primitive revelation. Thus Newman finds that everything falls into place. Just as all truth proceeded from the one God and revealer—including the truth still discernible in the heathen world—so too one can still refer it back to him as to its "one common origin".[17]

The special qualities of pagan tradition make it possible to distinguish it from the ecclesiastical, that is, from Jewish and Christian tradition, of which we shall speak below. The sense in which it is possible and necessary to speak of a tradition of revealed truths even among pagans has already been noted. There exist "the scattered fragments of those original traditions which might be made the means of introducing a student to the Christian system".[18] This was admittedly the method of the first missionaries[19] and of the Fathers.[20] But pagan tradition, even as far as it went, lacked the all-important authentication. "No people . . . has been denied a revelation from God, though but a portion of the world has enjoyed an authenticated revelation".[21] For lack of proper authentication, tradition among the pagans appears as a "vague and uncertain family of

[17] *Ibid.*, p. 170.   [18] *Arians*, p. 86.

[19] Cf. the starting-points used in the New Testament, e.g. Acts 2:14–36; 3:11–26; 7:1–53; 17:22–31 etc.

[20] Cf. Clement of Alexandria, *Stromata*, VI, 648 (quoted in *Arians*, p. 81, note 7): "Greek philosophy was a sort of dispensation of its own, given to be a stepping-stone to the Christian philosophy".

[21] *Fifteen Sermons*, II.

truths".[22] They came from God, "but still they were but rumours, they were vague, uncertain, and defective",[23] "they never attained the dignity and stability of doctrines— they had no authority".[24]

The result of these considerations is the conviction"that the Church of God ever has had, and the rest of mankind never has had, authoritative documents of truth, and appointed channels of communication with Him".[25] Tradition's proper and essential place is, therefore, a community founded and protected by God. The Church is such a community, both the Church of the ancient covenant of the Israelites and the Church of the new covenant of Christians.

2. *The Israelites*

In the religion of Israel, tradition undoubtedly was of very great importance, since the divine revelation, as it had existed from the beginning,[26] was entrusted to the charge of the people of Israel. Thus the doctrine transmitted in Israel is the norm by which pagan traditions are judged. "In truth, Judaism was, in God's mercy, the correction, the restoration, of those degenerate and corrupt religions".[27] In other words, the various pagan religions of pre-Christian times are off-shoots of the one religion of the patriarchs of

[22] *Arians*, p. 81   [23] *MS* A 17, no. 110, p. 2.   [24] *Ibid.*
[25] *Arians*, p. 80.   [26] Cf. *Grammar of Assent*, p. 431.
[27] *Subjects of the Day*, p. 214.

Israel, even though the pagan religions were corrupt and disfigured versions of it.[28]

This prerogative of the Israelite tradition is based on Israel's position as the people of the ancient covenant. It was because of the covenant that God bestowed upon Israel the privilege of bearing for many centuries true and uninterrupted witness to revelation.[29] Loyalty to the tradition of the ancients appears as an essential necessity, from the very nature of the case. It is merely the confirmation of an antecedent probability when reverence for antiquity takes on the nature of a commandment.[30] Newman sees in David a characteristic representative of Israelite attitudes and purpose: he comes midway between Abraham and the promised seed,[31] and his "peculiar excellence is that of fidelity to the trust committed to him";[32] and there were many like him who guarded faithfully the tradition of the fathers. But there were other types of men under the Old Testament among the Israelites to whom revelation had been entrusted to be preserved and handed down. There was also "the tradition of Pharisees",[33] whose religion showed itself in upholding formally what they did not fulfil inwardly. For them "perfection lay in merely answering the demands of society",[34] and thus, by concentrating on externals they "misused the traditions".[35]

God protected his revelation in Israel by sending his

[28] Cf. *Parochial Sermons*, V, p. 170; *Subjects of the Day*, p. 98.
[29] Cf. *Grammar of Assent*, p. 433.
[30] Cf. *Parochial Sermons*, VII, p. 253.
[31]Cf. *Ibid.*, III, p. 45.   [32]*Ibid.*, III, p. 52   [33]*Ibid.*, II, p. 105.
[34] *Occasional Sermons*, p. 22.   [35] *Ibid.*

people leaders, teachers and prophets. They did not merely safeguard the truth against distortion and corruption by their warnings and reprimands: they also appeared as bearers of new revelations and of truths which enlarged and added to the ancient deposit. This is one difference between the old dispensation and the new. Throughout the ancient covenant, there was a growth in revelation, not merely from within, but from without. "The doctrines proposed to (the Israelites) by Almighty God, the objects of their faith, have not been always the same, but as time has gone on, there has been a depth and width and height and breadth given to the divine message".[36] Thus it is clear "that there has been an increase of light in the Church, that there has been a progressive development of the gospel, that the Jews appear to have known more than the old patriarchs".[37]

The difference thus indicated between the Church of the ancient covenant and the Church of Jesus Christ, in its relationship to the transmission of revelation, may be seen more fully and clearly when we envisage their common foundations. Their unity lies in their author, who is the same God of the covenant who gives them the same truth. This central unity was expressed in the fact that "Christianity became the legitimate heir" of Judaism,[38] in the fact that in a certain sense Judaism "is the beginning of Christianity and its evidences",[39] or in the fact that Old Testament doctrine attained its "fulfilment, the due development"[40]

[36] *MS* A 17, no. 111, p. 1 (from a sermon of 23 October 1825).

[37] *Ibid.*, p. 3.   [38] *Grammar of Assent*, p. 439.

[39] Cf. *MS* A 16, 4 I, p. 144.

[40] *Parochial Sermons*, II, p. 185.

in the New. Thus the traditions of the Jews were not abrogated like those of the pagans. They were rather transformed into the Christian tradition. In other words, "Christianity was, and was not, a new religion"; it was "at once the same and not the same" as Judaism.[41]

The contrast is not merely the fact that the incomplete has been fulfilled, [42] that "the promises to Israel are really accomplished".[43] A basic difference, "the great peculiarity of the Gospel",[44] is that the promise is fulfilled by the special presence of the Spirit, who bestows on the doctrine and the doctrinal tradition of the Church of the new covenant an incomparable certainty, breadth and duration. The claim to universality and catholicity was an evident and necessary consequence.[45]

3. Christians

a) The orthodox

The community of the new covenant which Christ instituted is the heir to the old, which it also completes and fulfils. It possesses, therefore, by virtue of its very foundation and constitution "an indefectibility in existence",[46] so that it can never be supplanted by a new form of the

---

[41]*Ibid.*, p. 186.   [42] Cf. *Discourses*, p. 248.

[43] *Subjects of the Day*, p. 196.

[44] *MS* A 17, no. 118, p. 2; cf. *Subjects of the Day*, p. 172.

[45] *Discourses*, p. 248: "it became universal".

[46] *MS* A 18, 20.

covenant. The Church of the New Testament "will continue to the end of the world".[47]

Thus the Church was created in a state of perfection, so to speak, because its task is "to be like a city on a hill, a witness": the Church is "the witness to God".[48] One of the reasons why "a visible Church was instituted . . . was to prevent the loss of the best of his gifts",[49] or, to put it positively, "to preserve purity of doctrine".[50] For this end, it was made "inflexible and rooted in its traditions"[51], so that Christians could always give testimony to the true doctrine of revelation. For the same reason, it was endowed with "infallibility in teaching, authority in ruling".[52] Thus it is empowered, with the help and guidance of its divine founder,[53] to protect, preserve and expound the divine

---

[47] Cf. *Essay on Development* (2nd ed.), pp. 203–7: "Chronic Vigour"; cf. *MS* C 5, 1: "It began even in paradise, when God himself promised a Saviour born of a woman, and it has gone on developing, notwithstanding all obstacles and all endeavours of enemies to extirpate it— even to the present day, and will continue to the end of the world. It is Catholic also being found in all parts of the earth" (from a sermon of 25 February 1874).

[48] *MS* A 50, 2, no. 122, p. 5; *MS* A 29, 4.

[49] Cf. *MS* A 50, 2, no. 122, p. 5.

[50] *Ibid.*, no. 157, p. 12: "Thus we have seen that in the days of the Apostles there was a systematic form of Church government among Christians. And why was this? . . . To preserve purity of doctrine". On this sermon of 19 November 1826 Newman wrote the comment on 10 December 1857: "This is one of the first, if not the first declaration I made of High Church principles".

[51] *Lectures on Difficulties*, II, p. 311.

[52] *MS* A 18, 20.   [53] *Lectures on Difficulties*, II, p. 322.

doctrine. Hence Newman says that "the Catholic Church is the One Authoritative Oracle of God, the One Ark of Salvation".[54] Its doctrine is "authenticated",[55] its tradition of teaching is "authoritative and permanent".[56] In the words of the Apostle, it is "the pillar and the ground of truth".[57] Christ's Church of the new covenant is thus fitted, after the closing of revelation,[58] to guarantee its inner growth in just and unadulterated forms.

These remarks were meant merely to delineate the work of the Church from outside, as it were, and to distinguish it from other institutions. We now proceed to examine Christian tradition from within, to ask what its organs, its object and its modes of procedure are, so that we can see precisely the answer which Newman gives to these questions.

b) *Heretics*

But before we consider tradition as it appears in the Catholic Church, the function of heresy and its tradition outside the fellowship of the Church must first be discussed.

According to Newman, the attitude of the Christian to traditional doctrine is decisive for the orthodoxy of his

---

[54] *Newman-Keble Correspondence*, p. 31, note 3.

[55] *Lectures on Difficulties*, II, p. 322.

[56] *Ibid.*

[57] 1 Tim 3:15, quoted in *Lectures on Difficulties*, II, p. 322.

[58] *Lectures on Difficulties*, II, p. 327: "no simply new truth . . . since St John's death".

faith. To hold to the scriptures and to argue from them is not enough. Decisive is the fact that Christians "commit themselves to immemorial tradition".[59] Just as the Arians appealed to scripture and disdained tradition,[60] and hence separated themselves from the fellowship of the Church, so too, in the light of this criterion, divisions have constantly occurred in the history of the Church.

It was the example of the Anglican Church that showed Newman that where the authentic and authoritative tradition is rejected, a local ecclesiastical tradition of a peculiar nature soon slips in from outside, and so characterizes the heresy.[61]

The retention of the true, traditional revelation is incompatible with the introduction of new doctrines: "the very characteristic of heresy is this novelty and originality

[59] Cf. *Essays Critical*, I, p. 128.

[60] *Ibid.*: "The handful of bishops who supported Arius did not make any appeal to any uninterrupted tradition in their favour. They did but profess to argue from Scripture and from the nature of the case". At the beginning Newman could find no sure way of settling this question (cf. *Mozley*, II, p. 113: "Scripture proves and the Church teaches"), but later he clearly took tradition as the norm. Thus he writes, in a marginal note in his own original text of *Apostolical Tradition*, p. 335: "Bishop Taylor seems to contradict part of this doctrine, saying: there was then no heresy, that pretended any foundation from Scripture, but from Tradition many (Dissuasive, Vol. 10, p. 419). I believe Athanasius says, Orat. In Arian 1 . . . that the Arians were the first who appealed (relied?) on Scripture" (*MS* A 13, 2).

[61] See *Lectures on Difficulties*, I, pp. 6 f., 39, 109, 132 f., 140–3, 151, 193, 219 etc.; *Present Position of Catholics*, pp. 53, 62–67, 71, 178 etc.

of manifestation".[62] Nor can it tolerate the anachronistic reproduction of a stage of primitive Christianity, which is held to be authoritative for one reason or another.[63] The tradition of the deposit of faith must not try to leap across the centuries, but must reach each age in a continuous line of descent down the ages. To disregard this principle is to fall inevitably into error and distortion of the truth.

Not all the traditions, of course, of a separated Christian community need be false. On the contrary, "there is no religion which has not retained in it some traditions of the one true faith which the Catholic Church teaches in fullness and unity".[64] The separated Churches live by these partial truths. The duration of heresy is likewise limited. In affirming this, Newman is merely giving the obverse of the famous axiom, *"Veritas praevalebit"*,[65] understanding *"veritas"* as the truth of revelation correctly transmitted. The sundered group faces the destiny of all things composite: since its doctrine is a combination of divine and human elements, it must fall apart sooner or later, it is doomed from the start. "The course of heresies is always short".[66] Even the fruit they bring forth is only an illusion, and their error, "if it does not result in death, is resolved into some new, perhaps opposite, course of error",[67] equally fragile.

---

[62] *Essay on Development* (2nd ed.), p. 351.

[63] On archaistic tradition, see J. R. Geiselmann in M. Schmaus, ed., *Die mündliche Überlieferung* (1957), pp. 184 ff., 188 ff.

[64] *MS* B 3, Box II, 1.

[65] *Via Media*, II, p. 342, note on par. 6.

[66] *Essay on Development* (2nd ed.), p. 204.   [67] *Ibid*.

91

IV. THE TRADITION OF THE WORD OF REVELATION IN THE CHURCH

IT HAS already been explained that for Newman, the Holy Spirit founded and guides the Church in such a way that the truth of revelation is preserved within it.[1] Further, this community is, within the framework of human history, the most perfect instrument[2] for handing on to all men for all time the revelation completed and closed in Christ. Thus Newman can say in his essay on the Church that it is the community to which "the revealed word of God was committed, to be proclaimed by it".[3] From the point of view of the *verbum revelatum*, therefore, the essential task of the Church, as the "coetus praedicantium", is the preaching[4] or the handing on of the word;[5] and its special characteristic is the infallibility of this tradition.[6] Thus God has made the Church to be in a special way "the treasure and the channel of his grace".[7] The Church presents the word of God to man in a way which is always valid for each age. It might even be affirmed that "the word of the Church is the word of the revelation".[8] The "care of revelation and its interpretation"[9] has been confided so fully

---

[1] See pp. 75–79 above.

[2] See pp. 87 f. above.

[3] Cf. *MS* A 18, 20 (appendix, no. 4): "coetus cui traditur verbum revelatum, ut ab eo praedicetur".

[4] *Ibid.*   [5] *Ibid.*   [6] *Ibid.*

[7] *Parochial Sermons*, III, p. 220.

[8] *Grammar of Assent*, p. 153.   [9] *Ibid.*

to the Church that one can say with certainty that God made the Church for the transmission of revelation.[10] According to a fundamental principle of the Catholic religion, "the Church is the infallible oracle of truth".[11]

1. *The faith handed on*

a) *The deposit*

Christ entrusted the truth, revelation, to his Apostles. These handed it on in word and in writing, by their lives and by their teaching. Thus the gospel faith lives on as a definite deposit in the Church, "the same in every age",... "such as admits of being received, preserved and transmitted".[12] This deposit of faith, or the content of revelation, is not a more or less "accidental deduction from Scripture",[13] but an independent "substantive teaching"[14] which was received orally from the Apostles. The doctrine can first be negatively defined. It is not a collection of rules, and it is not a fixed list of articles of faith clearly drawn

---

[10] Here we have the same sort of ideas as were developed by J. A. Möhler, who held that the Church as a community comes to be by means of tradition: "Without tradition there would be no doctors of the Church and no Church, but only individual Christians; no certainty and security, but only doubt and probability" (*Symbolik*, 1873, p. 363).

[11] *Grammar of Assent*, p. 153.

[12] *Parochial Sermons*, II, p. 156.

[13] *Essays Critical*, I, pp. 125 f.   [14] *Ibid.*

up.[15] It should rather be compared to a philosophical system. It is a "divine philosophy", a system of thought,[16] and the nature and properties of the deposit are in keeping with this. If it is to be handed on, its spirit, its inner organic connexions, must be handed on. To know it, one must have experienced its whole atmosphere. It is handed on the way a philosopher hands on his doctrines to his followers, by "life-long contact".[17] If the learner has properly grasped the whole, or even part, that is, if he knows the true spirit of the system, he will himself be able to reach other parts.[18] Hence tradition can never really be committed fully to writing,[19] because it is something living. It remains inexhaustible in spite of all efforts to sound it, because with each new question that arises in the course of history, new aspects and connexions are brought to light, new conclusions are drawn. And "all these deductions are true, if rightly deduced . . . and therefore in one sense they are a portion of the deposit of faith or *credenda*",[20] they were already included in the great system of the divine philosophy.[21] Though they have newly

[15] See p. 60, note 64.

[16] *Ibid.*, note 66.

[17] *Essays Critical*, I, p. 126: "a life long contact between master and scholar".

[18] See p. 59, note 62.

[19] *Essays Critical*, p. 126: "too vast, too minute, too complicated, too implicit, too fertile, to be put into writing, at least in times of persecution".

[20] *Grammar of Assent*, p. 147.

[21] Cf. *Gregorianum* 39 (1958), p. 595; *ibid.*, 14 (1935), p. 418: "proprie non esse nova",

appeared, they are not really new. The deposit is better and more profoundly grasped from age to age, and though it remains unchanged, it is handed on as the fullness of divine revelation to the end of time.

b) *The Creed*

What has been said in general about the deposit of faith in the Church, may be applied in the concrete to the creeds, especially to the Apostles' Creed. Newman often treats the Creed in a wide sense as the equivalent of the deposit.[22]

The Apostles' Creed goes back to the Apostles;[23] though they did not compose it themselves personally, it is as clearly apostolic as any epistle of St Paul is Pauline.[24]

[22] *Via Media*, I, p. 218; *Gregorianum* 39 (1958), p. 595; *Essays Critical*, II, p. 6.

[23] *MS* A 29, 7 (transcription), p. 9: "for the Creed itself, it was made by the Apostles, but not written by them. As time went on others wrote what they had been taught by word of mouth". In a discourse of 21 February 1858, preserved in a transcription (*MS* C 5, 1), Newman discusses the twelve parts of the Creed and the usual reference found therein to the twelve Apostles: "This sub-division gave rise to an idea which was very generally believed among the faithful, that this Creed was composed by the Apostles themselves after the day of Pentecost, and before each went to his allotted sphere of labour . . . it does not seem to be well-founded. For those who examine the records left us of the early Church, find that each separate Church had its own Creed— in substance the same as the one now called the Apostles' ".

[24] *MS* D 6, 1: "Nay to a certain point, i.e. as far as the articles of the Creed go, no guide can be surer than Tradition. The Apostles' Creed is a document as surely apostolic as far as the matter of evidence is concerned, as one of the epistles of St Paul's."

We could add *a posteriori* that the Creed could only be genuine matter of faith at all, if it comes from the Apostles themselves: "because nothing can be of faith, nothing is revealed, except what comes from His Apostles".[25] For the same reason, it is evident that the ultimate author and giver of the Creed is the Holy Spirit: "these articles may be said to be his work".[26] Thus the apostolic tradition of the first centuries comes to us in the form of the Creed.[27]

As to its content, "the Creeds contain the catalogue of Christian doctrine ranged in order"[28]: "the Catholic Creed as coming from God, is so harmonious, so consistent with itself".[29] It does not contain indeed the whole of revelation explicitly, but it has all the essential elements, "summing up in brief what the whole Scripture doctrine on the subject implies".[30] From its close connexion with scripture, it is clear that the condensed but systematic formulas of the Creeds can be expanded, explained and rendered more colourful, when the copious but disordered data of scripture are appealed to.[31] Since the various forms of the Creed are so brief, "it is not surprising that they need a

[25] *Sermon Notes*, p. 317, which continues: "No revelation since—once for all—as sacrifice etc."

[26] *MS* A 29, 5 (transcription), p. 1.

[27] *MS* C 5, 1 (transcription): "That it has come to us even from the Apostles' time and has not been compiled since".

[28] *MS* A 50, 3 (sermon no. 225), p. 15.

[29] *Discourses*, p. 176.

[30] *Justification*, p. 316.

[31] *Via Media*, I, p. 244: "The Creed, indeed, can be proved from Scripture, which in this sense is its foundation".

96

comment",[32] nor that scripture can supply this commentary. The legitimate interpreter, who can use this commentary authoritatively and hence give an explanation binding in faith, is the Church.[33]

The function of the Creed was to provide a brief rule whereby the catechumen in the early Church could learn what the Christian faith was as a whole.[34] Hence it was and is still meant to transmit to all Christians the content of the faith in pregnant form, so that they can know, believe, profess and defend it. It is thus also understandable that "each Church had its own creed", which contained the same deposit of faith[35] and also that the various succeeding creeds should display characteristic formulations corresponding to each new age.

The Apostles' Creed is the original. It underwent no changes, because none of its articles were attacked in the Church of Rome, where it was in use.[36] The Nicene Creed,

---

[32] *Fifteen Sermons*, p. 327.

[33] *Jager*, p. 370: "Le symbole des Apôtres est la confession du chrétien, l'Eglise est son légitime interprète."

[34] *Essays Critical*, II, p. 7: "This Rule was prominently insisted on".

[35] *Sermon Notes*, p. 319: "Each Church, then, had its own Creed, the same".

[36] *Ibid.*, p. 319: "The Nicene has additions because of heresies—consubstantial etc.; the Apostles' Creed, that of the Church of Rome, where heresy never was". Cf. St Thomas Aquinas, *Summa Theologica*, II, II, 1, 9 ad 2: "haec fuit causa quare necesse fuit edere *plura symbola*, quae in nullo alio differunt, nisi quod in uno plenius explicantur, quae in alio continentur implicite, secundum quod exigebat *haereticorum instantia*".

however, contains the word "consubstantial", to reject a
heresy.[37] The Creed of Ephesus would have contained the
formula "Mother of God", except that the Council of
Ephesus determined that it should not be added to any
further.[38] Thus the various additions made to the Apostles'
Creed still testify to the task which these creeds performed:
to supply "a certain fixed collection of chief articles of
faith", to be handed on orally, to be used as instruction and
as a profession of faith.[39]

c) *Dogmatic definitions*

The councils that came after Ephesus show that heresies
did not cease with the fifth century. New measures of
defence against false doctrine and explanations of the true
doctrine by new formulations proved to be necessary.
These formulas too belong to the deposit, in keeping with
their type of origin and the degree of authority which the
Church, which proclaims them, allots to them. They are
"a portion of the Catholic Creed" and are then called
dogmas.[40] These "theological dogmas are propositions
expressive of the judgments which the mind forms, or the
impressions which it receives, of the Revealed Truth".[41]
Their polemical origin has already been noted. However,
no dogma can be formulated unless it has behind it "a

[37] *Sermon Notes*, p. 319.
[38] *Ibid.*   [39] *MS* A 50, 1.
[40] *Lectures on Difficulties*, II, p. 315.
[41] *Fifteen Sermons*, p. 320.

primitive and uninterrupted tradition" to give it certainty, or unless there can be demonstrated for it "a high probability drawn from Scripture and Tradition".[42] The casting vote is given by the teaching magisterium of the Church, which has informed itself with regard to the source of faith.

The great divine matters at which the human spirit toils "are far from being encompassed by those propositions"[43] of dogma. It is certain that the deposit of faith handed on in the Church will be further involved in an endless process of growth. For divine truth may not remain abstract: it must be proclaimed in concrete form in each age for a given set of men. The fact of this growth, whose nature must still be investigated, is a proof of the life of the Church and in the Church.[44]

2. The organs of tradition in the Church

a) The teaching Church

(i) The Apostles

At the beginning of the great chain of tradition, which goes back to Christ himself, stand the Apostles, "the first founders of His Church".[45] As instruments of the Holy

---

[42] *Lectures on Difficulties*, II, p. 304.
[43] *Fifteen Sermons*, p. 332.
[44] Cf. *Apologia*, p. 5.
[45] *Parochial Sermons*, II, p. 306.

Spirit they were inspired teachers and the infallible bearers of revelation, with the special power of being able "to answer questions at once" and infallibly.[46] Revelation was closed with them, and since the death of the last Apostle revelation has not grown in the sense of being added to. But apart from such special privileges, the Apostles also held offices which were of indisputable consequence for the life and doctrine of the young community of the Church. They were all teachers (διδάσκαλοι) and governors (ἐπίσκοποι) of the Church, while Peter was the chief (πρῶτος) of the Apostles.[47] They were representatives of Christ as prophets, priests and kings.[48] The offices they held may be said to have been essential in the constitution of the Church.

The charismatic privileges of the Apostles, their extra-ordinary prerogatives, ceased with their death. But since the ordinary power which they exercised in their office was and remains so vitally necessary for the Church, it cannot have expired when the Apostles died. Newman sees here the verification of a principle which he counts among the rules of revelation: "The duration of any gift depends

[46] See p. 62, note 78.
[47] Cf. MS A 18, 20: "The Prerogatives of Peter", on which Newman gives the following points: "1. Change of name . . . 2. He is put first in the catalogue . . . 3. His walking on the waters . . . 4. His knowing the mystery of the Incarnation and sonship . . . 6. The two draughts of fishes marking the Church militant and triumphant. Bellarmine . . . 7. Our Lord appeared to him first . . . 8. Our Lord washed his feet first . . . 9. He prophesied his death . . . 10. He is chief in Acts 1–10.
[48] Cf. Parochial Sermons, II, pp. 301 f.

100

upon the need which it supplies. Such at least seems to be the rule of a Merciful Providence".[49]

The rule is then applied to the offices of the Apostles and used to establish the principle of the apostolic succession.[50] This succession, in the broad sense of the term, comprises not merely the transmission of Holy Orders and the other sacraments,[51] but also the inseparable transmission of doctrine, which was passed on "from hand to hand, from bishop to bishop".[52] One may, therefore, affirm that the genuine tradition of the faith is signalled and guaranteed by the apostolic succession.[53]

One of the most important elements in the continuity and stability of a society is that there should be a well-regulated succession to guarantee and preserve traditional rules and customs from generation to generation.[54] So it was in the heathen world, in the Greek city-state, in the Mosaic covenant: and so too it has been established in the Church of Christ. There is of course this difference, that in natural succession tradition is handed on from father to son,

[49] *Ibid.*, p. 306.
[50] See J. A. Möhler, *Symbolik* (1873), p. 331: "By the Church on earth Catholics understand the visible community of all the faithful, instituted by Christ, in which the work which he did during his earthly life to purify and sanctify mankind was to be perpetuated till the end of time, under the guidance of his Spirit, by means of the permanent apostolic office which he ordained, so that all peoples should be led back to God in the course of time".
[51] Cf. *Parochial Sermons*, VII, p. 238.
[52] *Jager*, p. 375.
[53] Cf. *Essays Critical*, I, p. 225.
[54] Cf. *Parochial Sermons*, VII, p. 239.

while in the apostolic succession it passes from generation to generation of the clergy.[55] And here another aspect of tradition comes to light, when we consider the origin of the apostolic succession. "As the separate successions of bishops in various countries have but one common origin, the Apostles, so what has been handed down through these separate successions comes from that one origin".[56] Tradition thus brings with it the marks of its origin and its unity, when we consider the path it has travelled down the centuries. As Newman says, following Clement of Alexandria, all the Apostles had *one* doctrine and thus *one* tradition has come down from them.[57]

(ii) The bishops

As successors of the Apostles,[58] the bishops always played a commanding part in Newman's theology. The Apostles themselves are present,[59] so to speak, in the bishops and hence the doctrine of the Apostles is also to be heard from them. Transmission of revelation from bishop to bishop had been the first form under which Newman had envisaged the possibility of an incorrupt doctrinal tradition.[60] Thus the bishops show the place of authority in the Church, and the supreme doctrinal authority is embod-

[55] *Ibid.*

[56] *Essays and Sketches*, I, p. 122.

[57] *Essays on Development* (2nd ed.), p. 258 (Clement, *Stromata*, VII, 17).

[58] *Parochial Sermons*, II, p. 401.

[59] *Ibid.*, IV, p. 177.

[60] *Via Media*, I, pp. 244–9.

ied in them, apart from that of the infallible magisterium of the pope, in which, however, they have a certain share.[61]

"The essence of all religion is authority and obedience".[62] The rightfully instituted authority is of the essence of the revealed religion,[63] and the bishops are the cornerstones on which rests authority in the Church. They are indeed only authoritative teachers, in so far as they attest, propound and apply the traditional doctrine. It is not their subjective opinion which is normative for the Church, but the true, objective and divine doctrine. Thus they are not masters or judges of revelation, even though they have a special position as its mediators. But they are the authorized keepers, guardians and teachers of the divine word.

There is no need to dwell on the fact that priests, according to their rank, reflect in their way the function of the bishops in transmitting the tradition. "Each circle of Christians has its own priest, who is the representative of the divine idea to that circle in its theological and ethical aspects"[64]. All Christian ministers, down to the lowest degree of orders, participate in the charge and are bound, in faith and love, according to their rank, "to preach and preserve the Gospel of Christ".[65]

[61] Cf. K. Algermissen, *Konfessionskunde* (6th ed., 1950), p. 216; English translation: *Christian Denominations* (1950).

[62] *Essay on Development*, p. 86.

[63] *Ibid.*   [64] *Catholic Sermons*, p. 119.

[65] *MS* A 50, 1, no. 354, p. 6: "First the frame of mind and the objects to be had in view by the Christian Minister.—This is signified by the words which will serve to suggest to us the two great motives under which we must preach and preserve the Gospel of Christ (Visitation Sermon of 28 August 1834). Cf. also *Subjects of the Day*, p. 227.

(iii) The councils

Synods of bishops have a special place as organs of tradition, and in particular the ecumenical councils.[66] Their decisions provide not merely "a witness to tradition"[67] but incisive, clear and instructive decrees, which are a confrontation of the doctrine of salvation with the actual questions of the day. Each of the bishops separately is a qualified witness of tradition, but when they are gathered in council, in union with the pope as the supreme witness and teacher, under the guidance of the Holy Spirit, the deposit is present to them in such fullness and clearness,[68] that they are enabled to give a true and correct decision. That this decision may be qualified as "infallible" depends on the pope alone: "the seat of infallibility is in him, and they are adjuncts".[69] Nonetheless, all the Fathers bring the weight of their local or national tradition to bear, and thus a council becomes an imposing manifestation of authority.[70] Worthy prelates, laden with the traditions and rivalries of their own peoples and their own types of piety,[71] allow themselves to be influenced by other Council Fathers and yet in the end, in their definitive statements, are guided by the spirit of the Church, in the Holy Spirit.

[66] Following Bellarmine, Newman distinguishes various types of council, cf. *Via Media*, II, p. 284, note 1; *Arians*, p. 468.
[67] Cf. *Essays Critical*, I, pp. 123–7: "The Council of Nicea a witness to tradition".
[68] *Gregorianum* 39 (1958), p. 596.
[69] Cf. *Lectures on Difficulties*, II, p. 371.
[70] *Apologia*, p. 265.   [71] *Ibid.*

(iv) The papacy

No matter how high the authority of the office-holders, their powers and activities will be useless if there is no supreme authority who has the final say, and if his decisions are not infallible. This truth follows logically from the structure of the Christian Church and the nature of its doctrine and of the transmission of the doctrine. The consideration was enough to make the Tractarians postulate an objective and absolute doctrinal authority,[72] though they did not neglect what is much more important, the proof of the institution of the office. Hence they called for complete obedience to their bishops, when they spoke *ex cathedra*.[73]

In an exposition of Newman's teaching on the infallible magisterium, we may start with his assertion that the needs of our day are the strongest argument in its favour: "where the human mind is so busy, its thinking so fruitful and opinions so diverse ", a supreme spiritual authority is necessary.[74] Revelation, which was given its first firm support in the inspiration of scripture, is given an interpre-

[72] Cf. *Newman-Keble Correspondence*, p. 300.

[73] Cf. *Via Media*, II, pp. 200, 398; *Essays Critical*, I, p. 264; *Apologia*, p. 107: "The Bishop is our Pope".

[74] Cf. *Essay on Development* (2nd ed.), p. 89; *Apologia*, pp. 245 f. When Newman speaks in this way, it must be remembered that in keeping with his characteristic way of thinking, he first demonstrates the antecedent probability (*Essay on Development*, 2nd ed., ch. II, sect. 2) and then the reality which chimes with it (*Essay on Development*, 2nd ed., ch. II, sect. 3).

ter and guarantor in the infallible teaching authority.[75]
There must be an authority if there is a revelation, but no
other authority exists except that of the infallible magisterium.[76] It is only by this gift of infallibility in the Church[77]
that the transmission of teaching from generation to
generation, by means of tradition, can ultimately be
justified.

Before the definition of 1870, Newman distinguished
the concept of the infallibility of the pope from that of the
Church.[78] They are in reality essentially linked. The
infallibility of the pope signals the place where the infallibility of the Church is embodied. Some Anglican theologians
admit a certain indefectibility of the Church,[79] but an
active infallibility in teaching and deciding doctrine, its
localization in a personal office, is exclusively Roman
Catholic doctrine. The supreme authority is not in a
position of isolation when it gives its decisions. It always

[75] *Stray Essays*, p. 7: "I answer that there are two such dogmas; one
relates to the authority of scripture, the other to its interpretation. As
to the authority of scripture, we hold it to be, in all matters of faith and
morals, divinely inspired throughout; as to its interpretation, we hold
that the Church is, in faith and morals, the one infallible expounder of
that inspired text".

[76] *Essay on Development* (2nd ed.), pp. 88 f.

[77] *MS* A 29, 4 (transcription in shorthand of Joseph J. Hadley): "and
therefore that teaching involves the gift to the Church of not being able
to err in those things which are Christian truth or Gospel".

[78] *MS* B 7, 4 (10 July 1866): "Since the infallibility of the Church has not
been defined, it must be defined, if anything on the subject is to be
defined, before we come to the infallibility of the Pope".

[79] See above, esp. pp. 19–24.

exercises its authority with "a tacit reference to tradition as the medium of its exercise",[80] though it is not bound always to indicate "the express channels or records of tradition".[81] In other words, even when the pope alone— without the solemn gathering of the bishops in ecumenical council—gives a doctrinal decision *ex cathedra*[82] in matters of faith or morals, he cannot act in isolation from the *Orbis terrarum*.[83] These considerations not only indicate the relationship of the magisterium's verdict to the Church, they also point to the source from which the living tradition flows. The relationship between the universal magisterium and the whole Church stands out clearly in the preparations for the definition of the last two Marian dogmas.[84]

[80] *MS* B 7, 4: "She (the Church) never exercises it without a tacit reference to tradition as the medium of her exercise of it—even though she does not, and is not bound to, mention the express traditions (channels or records etc.)". (Suggestion to Fr Ignatius Ryder, 24 June 1867).
[81] *Ibid*.
[82] On this point J. L. Murphy writes: "It was not apparently until Melchior Cano that anyone spoke of the ex cathedra statements of the Pope in the sense in which we understand it today". See *The Notion of Tradition in Driedo*, unprinted dissertation, Rome (1957), p. 312.
[83] *MS* B 7, 4: "Of course we must define the orbis terrarum. I mean by it that rounded circumscribed definitely distinct body, which has one polity, one organisation, one government, one administration".
[84] Cf. the encyclical *Ubi Primum* of Pius IX, 11 February 1849: "ut nobis significare velitis, qua devotione vester clerus populusque fidelis erga Immaculatae Virginis conceptionem sit animatus, et quo desiderio flagret, ut eiusmodi res ab Apostolica Sede decernatur'e Quoted by Newman in "Judgment of the English Bishops on th'.

As a comment on the nature of infallibility in the magisterium, we can appeal to a brief description given by Newman, when he says: "I believe the Creed (i.e. the Deposit . . .) was delivered to the Church with the gift of knowing its true and full meaning."[85] It is a characteristic feature of this knowledge that the Church gains deeper and broader insight into it "intermittently, in times and seasons",[86] "according as she is guided by her Divine Instructor".[87] And it is a further feature of this knowledge that it does not always present itself with the same clarity and distinctness from the beginning with regard to all its aspects. It often remains hidden and obscure "in the mind of the Church".[88] It becomes clear and distinct through the specific process of definition or declaration of dogma. Whether it be the pope *ex cathedra* or the Fathers and doctors in a general council along with him, they receive the necessary insight for the needs of the day, under the assistance of the Holy Spirit. Thus a truth of faith, which existed habitually in the mind of the Church in an obscure fashion, is transformed into a new type of clear and actual knowledge, which may be couched in the form of an articulate proposition.[89]

Royal Commission", *The Rambler* (May 1859), p. 122; cf. "On Consulting the Faithful in Matters of Doctrine" in *The Rambler* (July 1859), pp. 198–230. For the encyclical preparatory to the definition of the Assumption, cf. *AAS* 42 (1950), p. 783.

[85] *Gregorianum* 39 (1958), p. 595.

[86] *Ibid.* [87] *Ibid.* [88] *Ibid.*

[89] See the letter to Fr Flanagan, *Gregorianum, loc. cit.*

To sum up Newman's doctrine on the infallibility of the magisterium, we may say of the Church:

1. It is self-sufficient, just as any living thing is meant to be self-sustaining and self-sufficient.
2. It knows the truths of its faith by virtue of divine assistance.
3. For the same reason, it knows the limits of the deposit.
4. It will never be allowed to proclaim as revelation what has not been revealed, and what it proclaims as revealed is revealed.
5. It cannot do anything in word or deed to the detriment of the deposit.
6. It knows what views are profitable and useful to the deposit.
7. By the nature of the case, it cannot increase the deposit of faith.[90]

The infallibility of the Church, as the essential note of its magisterium, makes the pope the most important organ of tradition.[91] He possesses by divine right "universal, immediate and supreme jurisdiction".[92] This is what sets him

[90] *MS* B 7, 4; see appendix 5. Cf. the seven points in the *Apologia* (p. 250), written two years earlier.

[91] See p. 100, note 47.

[92] *MS* A 18, 20: "The Pope is the source of all jurisdiction. His jurisdiction is universal, immediate, supreme. He has no episcopal power over Bishops. This prerogative is jure divino".

109

above the other bishops, whose jurisdiction is confined to their own territory. But since the authoritative teaching power of the Church of Christ, as an exercise of office, is part of jurisdiction,[93] it is, by divine right, the ground of the universality of the infallible magisterium.

It was for this reason that Newman saw in the Bishop of Rome the centre of the unity of the Church and of its tradition, and consequently saw that the unity of the Church postulated his infallibility: "If unity is unity of faith as well as unity of communion, and again all ecclesiastical unity is founded on unity of faith, and if no one can compel unity of faith but as an infallible authority, it follows that the Pope must be infallible in faith".[94]

The function of infallibility, as Newman sought to define it, lay entirely in the direction of the traditional deposit of faith: "The Church's infallibility is *wholly* ministrative to the *depositum* . . . and does not exist except as far as she is *custos, testis, judex, magistra depositi*".[95] This description of the object of the magisterium is not arrived at arbitrarily or from subjective motives; it follows the inward thrust of the sources of faith, as they show themselves in the testimony of scripture and in the creeds, definitions etc. of tradition.[96] These are the sources from which the decisions of the magisterium are derived. They also provide its limitations. The revelation already given and handed down forms the boundaries which may not be

[93] K. Algermissen, *Konfessionskunde*, p. 216.
[94] *MS* A 18, 20; cf. *Mozley*, II, p. 285; *Essays Critical*, II, p. 24.
[95] *MS* B 7, 4; see appendix, no. 5.
[96] Cf. *Lectures on Difficulties*, II, pp. 318, 329 f., 359.

passed, and indeed, under the influence of the Holy Spirit, cannot be passed; for the Church cannot increase its deposit.

Here too Newman comes to speak of the other limits of infallibility, with regard to the person of the teacher himself. In discussing this problem, Newman follows the teaching of Cardinals Turrecremata[97] and St Robert Bellarmine.[98] He holds that all decisions of the pope which are not given in the exercise of his extraordinary magisterium, that is, which are not solemn *ex cathedra* proclamations of matters of faith or morals, are excluded from infallibility.

The organs and bearers of divine revelation, who are concerned with teaching actively the truths of faith, constitute the active tradition of the Church. With these organs in mind, Newman defines the Church as the "coetus praedicantium".[99] The predominant and all-pervasive feature of this portion of the Church, according to Newman's description, appears to be the function of service and the attitude of watchfulness. For this there are two reasons: the majesty of the *verbum divinum* on the one hand, and the absolutely serious regard due to the Christian personality of the adult layman on the other. It is, therefore, impossible to speak of the preaching and handing down of the word of God, without taking in the "coetus credentium", who are as important as the "coetus praedicantium" or "tradentium".[100] Newman does not here

[97] Quoted in *Ibid.*, p. 359.
[98] Cf. *Essay on Development*, pp. 86 f.
[99] See *MS* A 18, 20; appendix, no. 4.   [100] *Ibid.*

speak of active and passive tradition. One may take it that he thought of the passive testimony to the faith on the part of the laity as an extremely vigorous activity. He uses the terms of teacher and learner.[101] But here we must not forget that every teacher is one who has been taught, though the converse is not true, that every learner becomes officially a teacher of the other. In other words, every Christian, by virtue of his baptism, belongs to the "coetus credentium", whether he is priest or layman, and shares the duties of the faithful with regard to tradition. By virtue of ordination, however, the priest has specific duties beyond those of the layman in the community of the Church.[102]

b) *The Church that is taught*

No channel of tradition may be neglected: "We have been viewing the argument on its hierarchical side; the witness of the Christian people for the orthodox truth is not less striking."[103] All Christians are in fact responsible for the keeping and the guarding of the faith.[104] The teaching Church is certainly in a more fortunate position when the laity is informed and interested than when all live merely by *fides implicita*, which can easily lead to indifference

[101] *Ibid.*: "docens and discens".
[102] *Parochial Sermons*, II, p. 255: "An order of men has been set especially apart . . . Ministers of Christ".
[103] *Essays Critical*, I, p. 130; cf. *Arians*, p. 445; "On Consulting the Faithful . . .", *loc. cit.*, p. 230.
[104] *Parochial Sermons*, II, p. 255.

among the educated and to superstition among the simple.[105] And responsibility for the faith extends to the whole body of the faithful, even to the humblest;[106] it is a "duty which attaches to all of us, to avow, propagate, and defend the truth".[107] "All Christians are in one sense preachers, missionaries and promoters of missions, but as Christ would have them, under rule and authority".[108]

It was Newman's conviction that the faithful had always responded widely to this call and had given strong testimony to the faith.[109] "In all times the laity have been the measure of the Catholic spirit".[110] The historic example is provided by the fourth century, in which the faithful surpassed many of their pastors in courage and in zeal for the faith,[111] because the good sense of the people remained unshaken while the speculations of theologians led to disasters. On this Newman based his opinion that the "*fidelium sensus* and *consensus* is a branch of evidence which it is natural or necessary for the Church to regard or consult".[112] This instinctive faith of the people, the accord of the faithful on a matter of revealed truth, is one of the

---

[105] "On Consulting the Faithful . . .", *loc. cit.*, p. 230.

[106] *Lectures on Difficulties*, I, p. 146.

[107] *Essays and Sketches*, III, p. 95; cf. *Discourses*, p. 111; *Parochial Sermons*, III, p. 364.

[108] *MS* A 50, 2. A later introduction to sermon no. 267 of 7 November 1830.

[109] See especially "On Consulting the Faithful . . .", *loc. cit.*

[110] *Present Position of Catholics*, p. 390.

[111] *Arians*, p. 446.

[112] "On Consulting the Faithful . . .", *loc. cit.*, pp. 199–200.

organs of tradition,[113] though in a passive sense. It is an instrument of which the magisterium makes use and which is capable of bearing witness to the true apostolic tradition. Newman's theory has been confirmed by the popes, since they proclaim their doctrinal decisions as corresponding to the faith of the people,[114] and have regard to that faith as a witness to traditional doctrine: "but the matter of fact, viz. their belief, is sought for, as a testimony to that apostolical tradition, on which alone any doctrine whatsoever can be defined".[115]

c) *The law of testimony in the Church*

Each Christian has the task of being a true keeper of the faith: "God forbid that any of us in his own station and according to his own opportunity should have helped in the diminution and wasting away of those things which Christ and his Apostles have bequeathed to us".[116] It is a task, as we have seen, which is incumbent on the whole hierarchy and on the least of the baptized, according to his degree. "Till we feel that we have a trust, a treasure to transmit . . . we have missed one chief peculiarity in our actual position";[117] "Our Lord was witness of the truth"[118]

---

[113] *Arians*, p. 467.
[114] See p. 107, note 84.
[115] "On Consulting the Faithful . . .", *loc. cit.*, p. 199.
[116] *MS* A 50, 4 (sermon no. 474), p. 14.
[117] *Parochial Sermons*, II, p. 267.
[118] *MS* A 33, 1 (transcription), p. 2; cf. *Parochial Sermons*, II, pp. 302 f.

114

and so is every subject of Christ: "everyone who has received the truth is bound to propagate it".[119] Thus since the time of Christ and the Apostles, "truth still makes its way in spite of the darkness, passing from hand to hand. At length we have received it . . . God forbid that we should not in our turn hand it on".[120]

We must now try to see what, according to Newman, the basic laws of this testimony are. He points to very specific traits which should be found in the bearers of revelation, if they are to be authentic witnesses to tradition.

To give testimony, one must first know the truth. But revelation is not a simple set of facts and propositions which could be mastered by reason alone. It is rather the personal self-disclosure of God: "God's voice speaking",[121] which demands a personal response, where the whole person of the Christian is involved. He must be wholly open to the message and to the messenger who brings it: his voice, his look, his actions must influence and inflame the personality of the Christian.[122] The supernatural atmosphere of the traditional doctrine, its true "idea", its authentic image, must have penetrated him and pervade his mind and his heart. This is the only way in which he can be said to have grasped and "caught" it,[123] this is the only

[119] *MS* A 33, 1, p. 4.
[120] Cf. *Parochial Sermons*, I, pp. 293 f.
[121] *Parochial Sermons*, IV, p. 314.
[122] Cf. *Discussions*, p. 393.
[123] *Present Position of Catholics*, p. 325.

way of mastering tradition.[124] "For surely those only can preach the truth duly who feel it personally; those only can transmit it fully from God to man, who have in the transmission made it their own".[125]

Thus the personal factor plays a fundamental role in the tradition of truth, both in its reception and in its transmission. And the gospel has in fact "been upheld in the world not as a system, not by a book, not by argument, nor by temporal power, but by the personal influence of such men, as have already been described".[126]

The fact that Newman uses the word "heart" to describe his concept of the personal element undoubtedly helps us to understand his position. The heart is as it were the centre of the person. The heart is what finally counts, because everything is there, everything proceeds from it, good and evil. In the heart, therefore, is to be found "the light of divine truth".[127] "Thus the heart of every Christian ought to represent in miniature the Catholic Church, since one Spirit makes both the whole Church and every member of it to be his temple".[128] The witnesses to divine truth must let it speak from the heart,[129] and they themselves must "throw their whole hearts and souls into their duty".[130] This is the only way for Christians to reach and stir the

[124] *Ibid.*
[125] *Discourse*, p. 365.
[126] *Fifteen Sermons*, pp. 91 f.; cf. p. 75.
[127] *Parochial Sermons*, VI, p. 303; cf. pp. 304 f.; V, pp. 45, 126 f.
[128] *Subjects of the Day*, p. 132.
[129] *Parochial Sermons*, VI, p. 305.
[130] *Ibid.*, IV, p. 17.

hearts of others ;[131] for "only the heart speaks to the heart", language reaches only the ear.[132]

The second important quality of genuine testimony is the actual effective seriousness with which tradition is "realized" in the heart of the witness.[133] "Realizing is the very life of true developments; it is peculiar to the Church",[134] and it means that tradition is constantly being grasped more deeply and put into practice more effectively. It is essentially in the "realization" that the supernatural is known and that knowledge of it is carried further: "the more we do our duty, the clearer we shall know our duty".[135] The real and authentic encounter with revelation can only take place when man confronts the truth in his own heart.[136] The message received in faith becomes the object of adoration: the letter is brought to life, theory becomes reality, promise becomes fulfilment,

[131] Cf. *Grammar of Assent*, pp. 92 f.

[132] The motto chosen by the Cardinal for his coat of arms, 1878, "cor ad cor loquitur" seems to have been taken from St Francis de Sales, *Oeuvres, Tom XII* (*Lettres*), vol. II (1902) [this volume belonged to Newman's personal library]: "Il faut que nos paroles soyent enflam-mees, non pas par des cris et actions desmesurees, mais l'affection interieure; il faut qu'elle sorte du coeur plus que de la bouche. On a beau dire, mais *le coeur parle au coeur*, et la langue ne parle qu'aux oreilles".

[133] Cf. *Parochial Sermons*, I, p. 84; V, pp. 9, 14, 22, 27, 31 etc.

[134] *Fifteen Sermons*, p. 337.

[135] *MS* A 17 (sermon no. 85), p. 8 (20 June 1825).

[136] Cf. H. Breucha in *Newman-Studien*, I, p. 164; Franz Wiemann, *Die Theorie des realen Denkens bei Newman*. Unprinted dissertation, Munich (1958).

thought action, words become deeds.[137] This is what it means "to realize a truth".[138]

Thus the Christian is only a true witness for tradition when his faith has become devotion,[139] when he has "realized" his Christianity. It may, therefore, be said that such "realization" is a fundamental property of Christian testimony. And it is not merely a condition to be fulfilled by the Christian if he is to bear the light of divine truth in his heart, to grasp it personally and to deliver it onwards; realization of the truth of the gospel also leads intrinsically to personal holiness, the integration of all the qualities required in the witness. For tradition is "the tradition of Saints".[140]

There are a number of other qualities which go to make up this basic law of testimony; but they can all be more or less reduced to those already named and are all integrated, as has been said, in the holiness of the witness. They include faith and love. "Faith ventures and hazards",[141] because though "faith is an intellectual act", it is open to the mystery of revelation.[142] But faith is not living and authentic without love: "we believe because we love". "The safeguard of faith is the right state of heart . . . It is love which forms it out of the rude chaos into an image of Christ . . . *fides formata charitate*".[143] This love of the gospel

[137] *Parochial Sermons*, I, pp. 169, 171; cf. p. 308.
[138] *Ibid*. p. 84.
[139] *Lectures on Difficulties*, II, p. 26; cf. p. 53.
[140] *Parochial Sermons*, II, p. 257—"saints" used in the original sense.
[141] *Fifteen Sermons*, p. 239.
[142] *Ibid*.   [143] *Ibid*., pp. 236, 234.

is indeed just the heart's dedication to divine truth.[144] A Christian is one who can confess that he bears in his heart the love of truth.[145]

When he has realized the divine truth, the Christian comes to the conclusion which St Paul already put before his communities when he wrote "the foolishness of God is wiser than men" (1 Cor 1:25).[146] From such true and realized knowledge of revelation, the witness receives the proper norms and the incentive which enable him to renounce, on the one hand, all that would be detrimental to the truth and its loyal tradition, and to dedicate, on the other hand, all that he disposes of to the service of this doctrine.

The realization of his love and the conflict between heavenly and worldly wisdom bring the Christian into straits and tribulation. Suffering is another essential element of testimony in the eyes of Newman. If we are to be faithful witnesses, "we must be willing to suffer for the truth",[147] and this readiness can involve us in the ultimate witness, martyrdom: "martyrdom, that is, dying for a Creed",[148] for a truth.[149] If even the first martyr had failed to give loyal testimony, we might have seen "the Church

---

[144] Thus Newman can simply say of Balaam, whose obedience was without love: "He did not give his heart to God" (*Parochial Sermons*, IV, p. 28).

[145] *Subjects of the Day*, p. 286; *Parochial Sermons*, IV, pp. 309 f.

[146] *Parochial Sermons*, I, pp. 215 f.

[147] *Subjects of the Day*, p. 62.

[148] *Miracles*, p. 355.

[149] Cf. *Discourses*, p. 102, *Discussions*, p. 293.

perished, the gospel lost, Christ dead in vain".[150] The importance of suffering is that it "realizes" to the utmost, in certain circumstances, the readiness of the heart to bear witness.

The sum of all the qualities which make up the true witness is found in holiness. Truth and holiness are akin, and their relationship is manifested when they are put into living practice, that is, when they are "realized". And hence it comes about that the saint acts as witness for the truth of the gospel not only while he lives, but after his death, and gives this testimony to the world.[151]

Finally, since the saint is what he is only through grace, grace is the decisive force which makes the Christian a witness to the traditional truth: "Grace acting through suffering, tends to make us ready teachers and witnesses of truth to all men".[152]

We may close this section on the characteristics of testimony, which is so much in Newman's style, by an exhortation from one of his Oxford sermons which may serve as a summary of his thought on the matter: "Let us think it far too great a privilege, for sinners such as we are, for a fallen people in a degenerate age to inherit the faith once delivered to the Saints;

> let us accept it thankfully,
> let us guard it watchfully,
> let us transmit it faithfully
> to those who come after us".[153]

---

[150] *Parochial Sermons*, II, p. 42. [151]Cf. *Ibid.*, IV, p. 157.
[152]*Ibid.*, V, p. 309. [153]*Ibid.*, VI, p. 342.

3. The modes of tradition

a) The divine idea

When God gave his revelation to the world, he exposed it to two influences: that of human reason and that of time. Human reason and time have a mutual relationship of an intrinsic nature, and something must be said of both.

We have already spoken of the fact that revelation comes to us in the form of the deposit.[154] We may, therefore, take this notion for granted here, as well as that of the "sacramental" word.[155] This word, which is met with in the concrete in the deposit of faith, is called by Newman "the divine idea" when considered in the fullness of all its aspects. This idea is given to man from heaven originally[156] in the form, so to speak, of "one dogma committed to the Church, which is in essence the whole truth, as a seed the tree",[157] containing all the truths of revelation. Being supernatural in its origin, the "Catholic idea" is indestructible.[158] Human reason tries to penetrate this idea, and gains a knowledge of it which it formulates in propositions and

---

[154] See pp. 93 ff. above.

[155] See pp. 70 ff. above.

[156] *Przywara-Karrer*, II, p. 65; cf. *Essay on Development* (1st ed.), p. 93.

[157] *MS Letters* 18; cf. *Fifteen Sermons*, p. 366: "the Catholic idea, and in it all are included." Cf. J. A. Möhler, *Symbolik* (1873), p. 369: "Once the divine word became human faith, it had to undergo the fate of all merely human things. It had always to be accepted and dealt with by the forces of the human mind".

[158] Cf. *Catholic Sermons*, p. 118.

their correctives. Having drawn the necessary consequences and formed the necessary definitions, reason arrives at a whole theological system.[159] But its activity does not end there. The urge to know pushes it still further, and the growth of the spirit can never be checked.[160] The end could only be brought about by the object, if all its aspects were grasped in their totality, and the idea then fully comprised and comprehended in an adequate act of knowledge. But such a perfection of knowledge cannot be attained even with regard to the objects and systems of our own world and its reality. Even here there are always new possibilities to explore, new aspects to throw light on, new means for approximating to the essence of the thing itself.[161] Much less is it possible to have anything like complete comprehension of revelation, where human reason is confronted with the mysterious truths of the Infinite.[162]

The intellect which searches revelation must be proportionate to the object. Here Owen Chadwick notes correctly the difference between Newman and Butler: "For Butler, the agent of development was the reason, the informed and scholarly reason of the academic. For Newman the agent

[159] Cf. *Fifteen Sermons*, p. 329.

[160] *Loss and Gain*, p. 202.

[161] *Grammar of Assent*, p. 151; cf. Fr. Taymans, "Le progrès du dogme" in *Nouvelle Revue Théologique* 71 (1949), pp. 687 ff.

[162] Cf. *Fifteen Sermons*, p. 334: "For though the development of an idea is a deduction of proposition from proposition, these propositions are . . . in fact one and all only aspects of it".

of development was the reason and more than the reason, the reason plus the conscience or moral insight".[163] But there is more than this. The study of the word of God does not begin or continue on the level of an adequate grasp of its object, such as is possible to the reason in its purely natural activities, which may also be aided and corrected by moral insight. Reason begins by accepting the word of God in faith, and from that faith goes on "to investigate, and weigh, and define".[164]

The insights gained into revelation, when they are solemnly and authoritatively established, are called dogmatic definitions. They are nothing but "the fruit of the Church's contemplation of the Divine Idea".[165] The tally of these dogmas or definitions will never be complete, as long as human history runs its course. Men will be constantly gripped by the divine idea and led to further insights. As these insights are compared with one another and contrasted with the idea, new consequences will always

[163] Cf. the remarks of Newman's disciple, Fr Ignatius Ryder, in a "Letter to William George Ward", of which excerpts are quoted in *JTS*, new series, 9 (1958), p. 326: "I do not suppose that unassisted human reason can always verify the process; because the full force and significance of the divine premiss can seldom be more than partially comprehended".

[164] In *Fifteen Sermons*, XV, p. 313, Newman uses the principle of "fides quaerens intellectum" to contrast the attitude of Mary with the unbelief of Zachariah: "thus she symbolizes to us not only the faith of the unlearned, but of the doctors of the Church also, who have to investigate, and weigh, and define".

[165] *M. Ward*, pp. 351 f.

ensue.[166] "The human mind cannot reflect upon that idea except piecemeal",[167] and this limitation is the cause of the multiplicity of dogmas.

The relation of doctrinal propositions about the idea to the idea itself must be examined more closely. The contrast between a closed revelation, which has been given once and for all, and the constant growth of dogmatic definitions is obvious. Newman sees these truths as new formulations of the idea, which also give new knowledge of the content under certain aspects, but express only what was already contained in the idea: "development being evidently the new form, explanation, transformation, the carrying out of what in substance was held from the first".[168] The relationship of the new definitions to the ancient truths is "homogeneous, cognate, implicit"[169]—and, we may add, each new formulation means progress in the knowledge of the reality of revelation.[170]

All definitions take place in time, which is one of the coordinates of revelation, as indicated above. Time is not

[166] Walgrave, *Développement*, pp. 188 f.: "L'évolution sociale d'une idée a donc pour cause première: la lutte et la reconciliation des aspects variés". "Le deuxième facteur du développement est le milieu".
[167] *Fifteen Sermons*, p. 331.
[168] *Lectures on Difficulties*, II, p. 314. O. Chadwick obviously finds difficulties in the use of the word "new" in Newman's writings.
[169] *Apologia*, p. 253.
[170] Cf. *Via Media*, II, p. 32. Cf. K. Rahner in *Wort und Wahrheit* (1950), p. 179: "We Catholic theologians hold that in principle each and every one of the dogmatic formulations which are binding on our faith is capable of improvement (without being false) and can be replaced by a better one".

124

merely the medium in which revelation arrives, it is also the medium through which it is grasped. Time is necessary if a great and complex idea is to be known: it is "remarkable how Scripture opens, as time goes on. New things come out of it . . . In truth, there are so many objects, and the human mind so weak, and it cannot be taken in all at once".[171] The whole of time will be necessary to take in even one important part of the divine idea, and this important part which is grasped "in the lapse of time"[172] is such knowledge of revelation as is necessary in each age for the salvation of the individual and of the Church. Time is "the great Innovator who creates new influences for new emergencies",[173] allowing new knowledge to come about in theology, so that men may be given new answers to meet their needs. The laws of the human mind are such that to refuse to go beyond the theological understanding of revelation, which was valid at one particular time, would be just as unhistorical as the effort to link up directly with the primitive community itself.[174] The ancient deposit and

[171] *Lectures on Difficulties*, I, p. 392; *Essay on Development* (2nd ed.), pp. 29 f.; cf. *MS* A 16, 4 II, p. 18.

[172] Cf. *Parochial Sermons*, VII, pp. 1–12, "The lapse of time".

[173] *Fifteen Sermons*, p. 128.

[174] Cf. *M. Ward*, p. 445: "the laws of the human mind made development of an idea the only alternative to its corruption or disappearance." Cf. Franz v. Baader: "The paradox of all life is that if it is to be true to what is ancient, it must not confine itself to it." (*Werke*, 1828, VIII, pp. 16 f.)

its development in the course of time must always be kept in mind, and must be voiced anew in the preaching of each age. Thus time, as it provides opportunities for the bearers of revelation, also imposes on them the great task of preserving the original revelation throughout the continuous historical process, which Newman calls development.[175]

b) *Being and becoming*

To understand Newman's doctrine of tradition, which culminated in his theory of development, it is not enough to adduce the *Essay on Development* and kindred writings. It is also necessary to bear in mind the general background of Newman's thought, from which this theory grew, if we are to avoid misconceptions.[176] The point is so important that it will be of interest to sum up once more briefly the main lines of the historical evolution of his thought.

In considering the tradition of the deposit of faith, which from the Anglican point of view meant only scripture and the interpretation of scripture, Newman began with a static concept of tradition. As he came to recognize the importance of the Creed, which was—from one point of view—formulated and handed on independently, he included it also in the static concept, and thus laid the foundations of the special concept of tradition in

[175] Cf. H. Bacht: "To accept tradition simply means that one is ready to take seriously the essentially historical nature of human existence." *Stimmen der Zeit* 4 (1957), p. 287.
[176] See Part II above, p. 48, note 37.

the episcopal tradition.[177] The static concept was sufficient in Anglican and Protestant theology. For Protestantism, which seeks its sources in the mind of the primitive Church, and the Anglican Church, which takes the first five centuries as classical and authoritative, disregard history to take as a norm the doctrine of those times which they evoke directly. The partial truth, which appears in these attitudes, demonstrates the permanent identity of the divine revelation. The doctrine of the Church of the present day must always be absolutely at one with the doctrine of Christ and must be able to show a clear and genuine continuity with it. It must have the same intrinsic and external structural laws. Newman never minimized the importance of this relationship. He maintained rigorously and watchfully the truth thus ascertained, throughout all the further stages of his thought.

But the fact of the static quality of tradition is only part of the matter. Two phenomena forced him to extend the concept. One was the manifold system of proposing, interpreting and applying the scriptures, to which Newman gave the name of "the prophetic tradition".[178] The other was the fact that the original formulations of the Creed of the first centuries were altered and enlarged. The close consideration of these facts led Newman to recognize clearly the dynamic element in tradition, from which two essential problems arose. The first was: what are the limits of this dynamism, that is, how long and to what extent does its activity leave the identity of revelation unchal-

[177] See pp. 46 f. above.   [178] See p. 47 above.

lenged? The second question is closely linked to the first: to what extent and in what manner are such consequences binding in faith? The existence of revelation, which cannot be futile if God is God, and the reality of the historical process, give part of the answer so fraught with consequences. But in addition, one must take into account the existence of a Church with the promise of the Spirit and the claim to teach. It may then be affirmed that revelation is the Catholic idea dwelling in the one Church, an idea too vital and forceful to stagnate, too well protected by the Holy Spirit to be subject to corruption.

This is the level on which the problems are to be solved. All consequences of the idea given in revelation, in so far as they are true developments and explicitations, are identical with the idea itself. They are not just the deductions of mere logic, "like an investigation worked out on paper".[179] It is the life of faith and not mere logic that has worked out these truths from revelation, and it is in life, and not just on paper, that the revealed idea has expressed itself. Thus the developments of revelation are as binding as the revelation itself.[180] To restrict this process of development to a ghetto

[179] *Essay on Development* (2nd ed.), p. 38; cf. K. Rahner, on the development of dogma, in *Schriften zur Theologie*, I, pp. 65 f. (English translation: *Theological Investigations* I, 1961): "The certainty of the truths believed by the Church as such is reached not merely by the logical explicitation of propositions, but by the power of the spirit in contact with the thing itself".

[180] Cf. Newman's "Manuscripts on Holy Scripture" in J. Seynaeve, *op. cit.*, p. 86: "He believes it, if it has really come down to us from Apostolic Tradition, and whenever it shall be made clear to him that it belongs to Apostolic Tradition".

of five or seven centuries, or indeed to any fixed period,[181] must under the circumstances be considered as a sin against the truth given by God. From this prehistory of the idea of development one can see how this theory of Newman's grew out of his own style of thought.[182]

The static and dynamic elements of revelation are, by their nature, and by reason of the medium of time, essential to the conservation and life of the deposit. To abandon either of them in favour of the other is to disregard history in one way or another. Either the origins are neglected, to make way for "enthusiasm" or the fanciful; or the continuity of history is not taken seriously, and an anachronistic "classicism" holds the field. Newman combined both elements in his theory of development.[183] Christopher Wordsworth could correctly say that the theory of development had many a Copernicus among Catholics, but had had to wait for Newman for its Newton.[184]

[181] Using the principle of regularity, one could argue analogously from the statement "What happened once may happen again" (*Miracles*, p. 103)–which suggests the continuation of God's miraculous activity–to the continuation of God's action in preserving revelation.

[182] Cf. Walgrave, *op. cit.*, p. 21: "La psychologie du développement c'est la croissance de son propre esprit".

[183] Cf. H. Bacht in M. Schmaus, ed., *Die mündliche Überlieferung* (1957), p. 54: "The problem is always this, that when revelation becomes known, it is in a certain sense unchangeable and in another sense changeable".

[184] Bishop Wordsworth of Lincoln (1807–1885) in *Letter to M. Gondon* (1847), p. 26: "Though the evidence is abundant and strong, that the theory of development is the only consistent theory of Romanism, yet it has never, I believe, been propounded so distinctly or marked out so

Newman was in fact the first to apply the concept of "development" to theology in England.[185]

c) *Correct development*

Tradition follows an evolutionary process. Thus in the medium of time, as the reason of believers does its conscientious work, the original revelation gives rise to a divine philosophy, a system of thought which continually expands to take in wider fields. A rich and vital idea, such as the Christian revelation, leads one to expect a rich and impressive development. The closer we are to the origin, the more it remains implicit. But the further we follow the course of time, the more we find revelation presented in fuller, distincter and more firmly defined concepts.[186]

The ultimate guarantee of the truth and validity of tradition is, as has been said, the Holy Spirit,[187] who is the decisive force in the infallible magisterium of the Church,[188] activating it and regulating it: "The real

elaborately as by the author of this volume . . . This theory has had many a Kopernikus among you, but he is its Newton". Cf. *DNB*, pp. 21, 925.

[185] Cf. Elliot-Binns, *English Thought*, p. 1: "The term development and the idea itself was first brought into connexion with English Theology by Newman".

[186] To avoid misunderstandings, it must be noted that it is not revelation itself that thus becomes more perfect, that is to say, its content, but the understanding and presentation of it. Cf. H. Bacht, *op. cit.*, p. 52; Lorinser, *Die Entwicklungslehre* (1847), p. 7.

[187] See pp. 75–80 above.

[188] See pp. 102–112 above.

authority behind the active development is that of the Holy Spirit, who works through the forces of growth which he has placed in the Church".[189]

Before we present Newman's theory of development, which is based on these principles, we may glance briefly at the rival theories, as H. Francis Davis terms them, which he had to contend with.[190]

1. The liberal view, according to which Christianity did not remain identical with itself anywhere in the course of development, but grew only by absorbing foreign elements, is one way of understanding development which Newman had to refute.

2. The effort to purify and correct the Catholic religion as it presents itself historically, by using the rule laid down in the Commonitorium of St Vincent of Lerins, is the second form.

3. The general Catholic solution, according to which all the doctrines which have appeared in the course of time were always present explicitly,[191] but cannot be

[189] Lorinser, *op. cit.*, p. 32. Cf. H. Schlier, *Bekenntnis zur katholischen Kirche* (1955), p. 176, who says that development "can only be understood as the self-interpretation of the 'primal' word of Jesus Christ through the Holy Spirit in the faith of the Church".
[190] H. F. Davis: "Is Newman's Theory of Development Catholic?" in *Blackfriars* (1958), p. 314. The hypothesis mentioned under no. 2 corresponds to the Via Media.
[191] See the view of J. S. Flanagan, quoted in *JTS* (1958), p. 327.

131

documented now on account of the *disciplina arcani* of ancient times,[192] is the third form.

Having discussed and rejected these three theories, Newman took up the question of the true criterion of development, in order to find a scientific method of justifying from without what was established in faith and from within through the magisterium of the Church. In other words, the notes given by Newman for the legitimate development of the idea were not meant to be a substitute for the teaching Church. With regard to the magisterium, they are rather aids for judging a development which claims to be authentic, to defend a truth after it has been defined and to demonstrate its derivation from the original deposit.[193] The seven rules which Newman put forward as the laws of explicitation[194] are all based on the general ontological principles of identity and contradiction.[195] The demonstration of the principle of identity and its transposition into "the concrete realities of the life of the spirit"[196] result in the principles of the "preservation of type", the "continuity of principle" and "logical sequence", as also in

[192] Cf. *Essay on Development* (2nd ed.), p. 29: "It is certain that portions of the Church system were held back in primitive times, and of course the fact goes some way to account for that apparent variation and growth of doctrine . . . yet it is no key to the whole difficulty".

[193] *Ibid.*, p. 321.

[194] See p. 55 above.

[195] Theodor Haecker in the epilogue to *Entwicklung der christlichen Lehre* (1922), pp. 460 ff.

[196] *Ibid.*

132

the principles of "chronic vigour" and of the orientation of the past to the future and of the present to the past.[197]

In the light of these obvious criteria each developed Christian doctrine can be seen in its intrinsic connexion with the original "idea" of Christianity. Thus, for instance, the cult of the saints appears as a straightforward development from the central truth of the Incarnation, under the aspect of mediation. It leads in direct consequence to the veneration of relics, blessings etc.[198] The sacraments are also a direct consequence of the central idea, under its sacramental aspect, that matter can be the vehicle of grace;[199] thus baptism can be seen to be a legitimate development, from which in turn developed confirmation on the one hand, and the sacrament of penance, the doctrines of purgatory and indulgences on the other.[200]

---

[197] *Essay on Development* (2nd ed.), p. 171.

[198]*Ibid.*, p. 94; *Ibid.* (1st ed.), pp. 36, 325 f.

[199]*Ibid.* (2nd ed.), pp. 401 ff.; cf. p. 368.

[200]*Ibid.*, p. 94. The later Marian dogmas should then be inserted into this line of development, as a few necessary considerations show. Corporeal matter, which was originally good, but was corrupted with the rest by sin, has been purified and sanctified once more by the work of grace. In the case of Mary, the sacramental principle did not need to develop into the doctrine of justification—on the basis of the doctrine of original sin. It had on the contrary been at work in its most perfect and privileged form, that of pre-redemption. Cf. the Bull *Ineffabilis Deus*, 8 December 1854: "intuitu meritorum Christi Jesu Salvatoris humani generis" (*Denzinger*, 1641). The privilege defined in this dogma then leads, on account of the sanctification of Mary's body, to the dogma of her bodily resurrection (i.e. her bodily assumption into heaven). Only then follow the holiness of her relics,

From the "cross relations",[201] which form another branch of developing revelation, the coordination between the individual truths or aspects and the total truth or primordial idea of revelation may be illustrated. Newman was clearly right in affirming that it would be the work of a lifetime to try to apply fully the doctrine of development to all the writings of the Fathers, to the history of controversy and of the councils, and finally to the decisions of the magisterium.[202]

We are here undoubtedly at the heart of Newman's doctrine of tradition. It is dominated by the thought of development, as is Newman's whole theology.[203] It uses the most universal principles of human thought, and was, therefore, reproached with lack of clarity and of rigour.[204] But it is able to embrace even the smallest movements and changes, in the concrete and in the abstract. The superiority of Newman's rule over that of St Vincent of Lerins, as a theory of knowledge and a guide to history, is all the more striking when it is applied to concrete cases. It is derived

the power of her intercession, the fact of the reverence paid her etc. (*Essay on Development*, 2nd ed., p. 402). Here then we have an example of the anticipation of doctrines which are to be expected later, such as Newman wished to indicate by the criterion of "anticipation".

[201] *Essay on Development* (2nd ed.), p. 94.

[202] Cf. *Ibid.*, p. 30.

[203] Cf. H. Fries in *Vitae et Veritati*, *Festschrift für Karl Adam*, p. 103: "Development is the characteristic feature of his theology in general".

[204] Cf. I. Döllinger's comment on Newman's theory of development "which can be stretched in all directions to take in whole continents of thought, like Dido's cowhide". (Quoted by H. Fries, "Newman und Döllinger" in *Newman-Studien*, I, p. 35).

to some extent from the formal aspects of the historical processes to which the revealed deposit was subjected, and hence it is a reflection of the life of the spirit[205] and can be applied throughout this field.

d) *The work of Antichrist*

The danger of revelation being corrupted has often been mentioned in these pages. We have not yet considered where this danger comes from. Newman described it exactly and gave it a personal name: "the work of Antichrist".[206] "This malignant principle" has already been at work since the time of the Apostles,[207] planning and working for the great "apostasy",[208] the destruction of the Church and her doctrine. Every human opponent of the Church in the course of history is in a way a precursor of the real, primordial adversary, "just as every event in this world is a type of those that follow, history proceeding

[205] Cf. the letter to Fausset (1838), where Newman gives this typical description of the influence of Froude's *Remains*: "They will make their way through the community, picking out their own, seeking and obtaining refuge in the hearts of Christians, high and low, here and there, with this man and with that, as the case may be". This phenomenological description shows how much Newman was preoccupied with the influence and spread of ideas.

[206] Cf. "Advent Sermons on Antichrist", *Tract* 83, in *Tracts for the Times*, vol. V, pp. 1–54.

[207] *Ibid.*, p. 6.

[208] *Ibid.*, p. 3 and *passim*.

forward as a circle ever enlarging".[209] Till the hour of Antichrist, the effort to make the power of evil triumph continues, with ever growing force. The longer time goes on, the more intense is the activity of the corruptive force, the greater the danger to the true doctrine. The Church always lives in the midst of corruption, because it lives in the world.[210] The world has its own principles in religious matters. They come from the adversary, who sows the seeds of error. "Error spreads and becomes an authority".[211] Its individual cells coalesce into an organism, relying on each other and on the whole, to find foothold and have permanence.[212]

Religious error lives outside the Church, even though it makes assaults on its members, but it lives from the true doctrine, as it "obscures or prejudices its essential idea".[213] It "disturbs the laws of development" and thus the development itself.[214] The results of such disturbances and perversions in the tradition of doctrine are corruptions and false doctrine.[215] This is the way the religion of the world, the religion of Antichrist, comes to be.

[209] *Ibid.*, p. 4.

[210] *Miracles*, p. 239.

[211] *The Development of Religious Error*, p. 7. This work grew out of a controversy with Dr. Fairbairn, who had accused Newman of scepticism. After an official answer in the *Contemporary Review*, Newman had the work printed for private circulation in 1886, to clarify his views on the matter. Cf. *W. Ward*, II, pp. 505–11.

[212] *Ibid.*

[213] *Essay on Development* (1st ed.), p. 63.

[214] *Ibid.*

[215] *Ibid.* "corruption".

Constant efforts must be made to distinguish the true doctrine ever more clearly and sharply from the false. The closer the coming of Christ draws near, the fiercer will be the conflict, which will reach its climax at the appearance of Antichrist. The clear contours of doctrine, which will by then be almost fully developed, will offer trusty help to the elect in the final struggle.

The tradition of error is doomed to destruction from the start, since corruption, in contrast to development, "is the breaking-up of life, preparatory to its termination".[216] The logic of things then allows us to draw with Newman some important conclusions. If the error is great and powerful, it cannot last long: "the worse, the shorter". If it continues on, it must be only a minor or mild corruption of the truth, which must disappear gradually.[217] A characteristic feature of collapse is the diversification of the error into many individual forms of error, each of which is threatened by the same fate. From this we may conclude that just as Newman is convinced of the unconquerable vitality of the truth, he is also convinced that error must perish.

These considerations might seem to suggest that all heresy was doomed to destruction *a priori* and, therefore, at least in the long run, need cause no anxiety. But this would be to overlook the fact that first of all, heresy presents an acute danger at any given moment of its existence, and then that it is a warning symptom of the endless activity of the Father of Lies and error. False doctrine calls for

[216] *Ibid*. (2nd ed.), p. 170.

[217] *Ibid*., p. 437; cf. p. 203: "the worse, the shorter".

watchfulness. Though every aberration from the truth bears within itself the seeds of death, no age will be without the danger of corruption, because Antichrist is never without precursors in the world. Tradition is, therefore, constantly exposed to danger and its bearers are engaged in an endless conflict. The history of the tradition of revelation and the forms which it takes are simply the ever-changing forms of the struggle between the Spirit and the Adversary, between the Church and the world,[218] between Christ and Antichrist.

V. DEFINITION OF TRADITION

1. *A specific difficulty in the definition*

It is not normally too difficult to arrive at a definition of a doctrine when its content has been described. The definition would be insufficient only if the description did not include all the aspects of the doctrine. Even then there would be two possibilities to explore. Either what was missing from the description could be taken into account in the definition, or some element must on principle remain obscure. This is in fact the specific difficulty which occurs when one attempts a definition of tradition in general and of Newman's concept of tradition in particular.

[218] Terence Kenny, *The Political Thought of Newman* (1957), p. 37: "All history is now a preparation for the coming of the Kingdom of God, displaying the ever new forms of the struggle between the Church and the World".

The tradition of revelation can be determined as to its starting-point, which for Newman was the beginning of human history.[1] The tradition of the full revelation, which was closed once and for all, begins with the end of inspiration, after the death of the last Apostle.[2] But this gives us only the beginning of tradition and its course up to the present. An essential part escapes us, whose impact we cannot foretell. We do not know what its future course will be and we cannot say what proportions it will take on in comparison with the past. Tradition will go on till the end of time, till all difficulties and controversies in doctrine are ended, till the "*lumen fidei*" is transformed into the "*lumen gloriae*".[3] When the end will come is unknown to us, and hence we do not know what period of time revelation has still to span[4] or how it may yet unfold and take shape. We do not therefore know whether a definition covers a large or only a small portion of the totality of tradition.

In spite of this difficulty, it is still possible to assert something essential about the nature of tradition. Its inner and outward structure can be determined. From the outlines thus drawn, we may suppose that we can gather something

[1] See pp. 80 ff. above.

[2] Cf. *MS* A 18, 20 in appendix, no. 4.

[3] Cf. Lorinser, *op. cit.*, p. 10: "This process of development begins on earth and ends in heaven in the beatific vision".

[4] Cf. *MS* A 29, 5, where Newman says of the Church: "He made it a long continued work. There is this peculiarity about it, we do not know how long it is to be, but he came at the beginning of it, and he will come again at the end" (from a sermon of 19 November 1876).

139

about the nature of tradition, and perhaps even be able to indicate what is essential in it. Such an assertion about the essence of tradition would point to something permanent about it which will enable us to take a step beyond the present, not only into the past but into the future.

2. *The formal aspects*

a) While the revelation of the new covenant could, until the death of the last Apostle, present and disclose itself in the form of inspiration, the time of tradition began after that. "Tradition now is the revelation".[5] In contrast to profane tradition, whose origin is often unknown[6] and whose truth is often questionable,[7] we can say of sacred tradition that "its matter is true and it is infallible".[8]

Newman divides it into "*locutio*" and "*scriptio*". Tradition as *locutio* means the purely oral transmission of doctrine, by preaching, catechizing, narrating and so on. *Scriptio* means both the transcription of inspired writings and oral statements and records of the words and writings of the Apostles.[9] These two (or three) forms of tradition exist in the Church not separately only but mixed. The

[5] *MS* A 18, 20 in appendix, no. 4.

[6] *Present Position of Catholics*, p. 46: "By tradition is meant what has ever been held as far as we know, though we do not know how it came to be held".

[7] *Ibid.*, p. 47: "but we are not content with it".

[8] *MS* A 18, 20 in appendix, no. 4. Cf. J. Pieper, *Die Tradition* (1958).

[9] *MS* A 18, 20.

140

sacred writings and the purely oral traditions and the oral traditions committed to writing exist in combination with one another. As such they give the answer to the question: what is tradition?

Newman is obviously taking tradition in a wider sense than is usually given the word in the strict terminology of the schools. In doing so, he affirms unconsciously and indirectly that the whole of revelation really comes to us in the form of tradition. Both of the witnesses to the faith are guaranteed by the same Spirit in the same magisterium.

b) By tradition in the strict sense of the word is meant the transmission "with dogmatic force"[10] of the doctrine received orally from the Apostles. It comprises the *locutio* and part of the *scriptio*, the part which was originally transmitted by word of mouth. Newman distinguishes the matter and the mode of tradition. Its matter is a "positive statement of belief",[11] in its mode it is "a statement which comes from the Apostles".[12] It can be positive, as when it makes a direct assertion of a doctrine; it can also be negative, as when it denies something, though even here something positive can be discerned.[13]

The traditional truths, negative and positive, are not always self-explanatory and never fully so: if their full import and depth is to be grasped, they need to be properly propounded and interpreted.[14]

If exegesis is necessary for the truths which came originally by writing, how much more so for those which have been delivered orally! Tradition has still another

---

[10] *Lectures on Difficulties*, II, p. 138.
[11] *Ibid.*, p. 141.   [12] *Ibid.*   [13] *Ibid.*, p. 139.   [14] *Ibid.*

feature in common with scripture. In both cases there are doctrines propounded explicitly and truths which are only implicit. An explicit tradition is a doctrine which is contained literally in the statements of tradition; the implicit tradition, however, is manifested in its force and efficacity.[15] Needless to say, implicit truths need explicitation, and explicit truths can give rise to deductions.[16]

c) The form of tradition just described does not exist in isolation. As has already been said, it is combined with written tradition and is inseparable from it. This relationship follows necessarily from the concept of revelation. The oral forms of the tradition of revelation cannot be isolated from the written forms, any more than one line of tradition can be isolated from another. For each item of tradition must either be "authenticated" by some external factor,[17] or be confirmed by means of a "cumulation of evidence" by other lines of tradition which testify to the same truth.[18] But even then a further proof of its origin may be desirable. Hence Newman is consistent in affirming that divine traditions always bring with them the demonstration of their truth, in the form of miracles or prophecies[19] or other signs.

Thus the tradition of the truth of revelation, which is "an elementary principle of Christianity",[20] always brings with

[15] *Ibid.*
[16] *Ibid.;* see on the whole question p. 59, note 61.
[17] *Present Position of Catholics*, p. 47.
[18] *Ibid.*, p. 48; cf. p. 52.
[19] *Ibid.*, p. 52.
[20] *Essays Critical*, I, p. 121.

it the necessary proof of its credibility. It has "an evidence of its Apostolical origin the same in kind with that admissible for the Scripture",[21] though the form may be different.

3. *The material aspects*

a) *The life of the Church*

Tradition, according to Newman, has various essential traits. Tradition is movement. The divine doctrine passes from mouth to mouth, from father to son,[22] from century to century. Tradition is development;[23] doctrine evolves and casts an ever wider spell upon men. Tradition is change and transformation in the sense of an organic, spiritual growth.[24] Tradition forms a unity: for all its variety, there is still a common origin, the parts are in mutual accord,[25] there is a single principle and a single doctrine, an essential, permanent identity of content. Tradition is an organic system: it is a large, comprehensive philosophy.[26]

[21] *Via Media*, I, p. 249.

[22] *MS* A 33, 1: "By Tradition we mean this: giving over from mouth to mouth, as it were, from father to son". Cf. *MS* A 29, 7, appendix, no. 7 c; *Essays Critical*, I, p. 122: "process of transmission and acceptance".

[23] See pp. 130–5 above.

[24] See p. 58 above.

[25] Cf. *Tracts Theological*, p. 116; *Essays Critical*, I, p. 127.

[26] Cf. letter to J. S. Flanagan, *Gregorianum* 39 (1958), pp. 594 f.; Newman and Perrone, *Gregorianum* 14 (1935), p. 407.

All these statements give an analogous description of what we sum up under the concept of "life" and of what Newman described as life. Life too is movement and brings with it a perpetual process of change and transformation.[27] Life too, in spite of its variety, is a unity with a corresponding principle, which works and reacts organically.[28]

It is, therefore, right and proper—in spite of all the reserves which had to be made at the beginning—to designate tradition as life, and to sum up, comprehend and define it this way. "What here is called life, the Catholic calls tradition".[29] The growth of tradition is "a law of life".[30] The developments which have occurred since the apostolic age are "a result and an evidence of spiritual life"[31] in the Church. Tradition is "the living voice, the breathing form, the expressive countenance, which preaches, which catechizes".[32] Tradition is more than the sterile repetition of a doctrine, less than rank proliferation; more than logical consequence, less than the random thrusts of the life-force. Tradition is life, moving and developing, governed by laws, sustained by personal forces, penetrated by the Spirit, enlisted by the Spirit, spinning the web of truth untarnished, a vast complexity which is still directed by the one idea.

[27] *Lectures on Difficulties*, II, p. 79.

[28] *Ibid.*, I, pp. 43 f.

[29] *Present Position of Catholics*, p. 326.

[30] *Lectures on Difficulties*, II, p. 356; the similarity between Newman's view and what J. R. Geiselmann, of the Tübingen school, calls "living tradition as norm of faith" is unmistakable.

[31] *Miracles*, p. 171.

[32] *Essays and Sketches*, II, p. 287.

144

b) *The conscience of the Church*

With the whole course of Church history in mind, one may call tradition the life of the Church. But that is only the first of the two essential aspects of tradition in the teaching of Newman. The second aspect of tradition, which is just as essential, concerns the Church as it continually grasps the faith anew at each given moment of history, assenting to the faith, drawing conclusions from it, giving decisions in accordance with it. If for no other reason, the first definition cannot stand alone because it could too easily give rise to misunderstandings. It is very broad and comprehensive. It can, however, still be clearly distinguished from the definition given by the Edinburgh Conference on Faith and Order in 1937, which likewise tried to describe tradition as life.[33] One clear difference is the ambiguity and readiness to compromise in the Faith and Order definition, which contrasts strongly with Newman's clear and definite shades of meaning. Another is the difference of origin clearly ascribed to tradition. According to the ecumenical conference, tradition, sharply distinguished from the truth of scripture, is born from the life of the Church; according to Newman it contains or is the word of God, and is constitutive of the life of the Church precisely in the sense of being its cause.

The second aspect is, therefore, necessary to mark the

[33] Edinburgh Conference on Faith and Order (1937). Cf. *ODCC*, p. 438. "It defined tradition 'as the living stream of the Church's life' ". Quoted by D. Jenkins, *Tradition and the Spirit* (1951), p. 15; cf. p. 17.

distinction and to give a fuller explanation of Newman's concept of tradition.

As has already been said, Newman considers that the word of God dwells and lives in the individual Christian as well as in the Church as a whole.[34] Just as the individual keeps and meditates the word of God in his heart, so too the Church in her "inmost sense".[35] For the "inmost sense" of the Church is nourished by the "deep sense" of the faithful, it is the instinct of faith in the Church, in which hearing and teaching Church are at one: "conspiratio pastorum et fidelium".[36] The instinct of faith is concerned with the concrete and personal truths of revelation, and should be described, in Newman's terms, as an "illative sense".[37] The "illative sense" of the Church would then be the principle of tradition. Since it is not a law like the rules of logic, but "the ratiocinative mind" itself,[38] the "illative sense" is to be identified with the act of tradition as a process.

This surprising conclusion is not all, however. The "illative sense" has been described as the intellectual parallel to moral prudence.[39] Applied to religious truths, as

[34] See p. 58 above.

[35] *Gregorianum* 14 (1935), p. 413: "fit sensus quidam intimus".

[36] *Ibid.*

[37] *Grammar of Assent*, p. 345 etc. Cf. Fr. Zeno, *Our Way to Certitude* (1957), pp. 19 ff.

[38] *Grammar of Assent*, p. 360.

[39] J. Artz, *Newman-Studien*, II, p. 236; cf. "Die Eigenständigkeit der Erkenntnistheorie Newmans" in *Theologische Quartalschrift* 139 (1958), pp. 194–222, especially p. 208.

happens when the illative sense of the Church is at work, it performs the function of the conscience and so would be identical with conscience. To come back once more to the formulation that the illative sense is to be identified with the act of tradition, we may now affirm that the act of tradition may be described as the functioning of the conscience of the Church.

This part of Newman's doctrine, which has already been recognized and formulated by H. Fries,[40] may be explained more precisely. It is concerned of course—to anticipate a restriction which must be made—with a metaphorical use of the term "conscience", just as all personal concepts are used in a transferred sense when applied to the Church.[41] But it is still possible to point to far-reaching analogies. Just as the individual conscience, which involves the whole personality, goes into action in a concrete decision about faith or morals, so too the Church with regard to the deposit of faith. Just as the Christian possesses in his conscience a firm and prescribed norm of conduct, so too the Church possesses in tradition an inviolable rule of faith, authoritative in itself, which it must keep. As conscience remains inexorably normative in spite of all the difficulties and wavering of the individual, so too the traditional heritage remains whole and true throughout all the struggles and sufferings of the Church, from within and from without. The limits to the analogy are clear, where the Church can no longer be compared to a person.

[40] Fries, *Tradition*, p. 143.
[41] *Gregorianum* 14 (1935), p. 413: "eandem . . . conditionem et historiam".

It might be asked whether this conclusion from Newman's premises may be regarded as Newman's own doctrine. The positive answer is given in the *Discourses Addressed to Mixed Congregations*, where it is made quite clear that tradition has the place and function of conscience in the Church. As conscience provides a legitimate and unerring norm when the book of nature is studied in view of the moral and religious good, so too tradition gives a legitimate norm for the understanding and explanation of revelation as a whole.[42] This is not the only example which may be quoted to show that tradition is the conscience of the Church. In a sermon of 14 August 1836 Newman says:

"In all ages, the Catholic Church is promised an instinctive perception of the Christian truth, detecting the grosser or the more insidious forms of heresy, though at a distance, as if by some subtle sense . . . and thus transmitting the faith of the Gospel pure and inviolate to the latest times".[43] The activity of this "subtle sense", by which the Church detects error and remains faithful to the truth, undoubtedly corresponds to the function of conscience in the individual, which warns him against faults and keeps him faithful to the good. That the conscience of the Church is infallible stems from the promise of the Spirit. We have here not merely a confirmation of what has already been said about conscience and the Church, but the indication of another

[42] *Discourses*, pp. 276 f.
[43] *Subjects of the Day*, p. 172; *Essay on Development* (2nd ed.), p. 361: "What conscience is in the history of an individual mind, such was the dogmatic principle in the history of Christianity".

distinctive truth which has already been touched on. While the individual can be untrue to his conscience, even though the conscience itself remains inviolate throughout, the Church is unfailingly loyal to the truth of revelation, by virtue of the divine promise. In other words, the Church's experience of Christian truth and its sensitive reaction to falsehood only partly resemble the activity of conscience. Man can reject the voice of conscience, because he is man, but the Church follows infallibly the voice of its conscience, because the Church is from God.

Thus tradition, as the conscience of the Church, shows the Church functioning as a whole in deciding on matters of faith and morals; it is the activity of the Church, in so far as it is inexorably moulded and guided by the deposit of faith which was given to it.

VI. SCRIPTURE AND TRADITION

THE problem which is so often discussed today, that of the relationship between scripture and tradition as channels of the faith, naturally held a large place in Newman's thinking, coming as he did from an Anglican background. His Oxford days give a clear picture of his growing sense of the importance of tradition, though he always gave scripture a privileged place. He sees the Bible as "God's voice to us",[1] as "the sacred book in which the fundamental truths (of

---

[1] *MS* A 17, no. 85, p. 2: "The Bible then is God's voice to us, and calls us as it called Samuel, to listen and obey."

religion) are contained",[2] as the key to the true meaning of the world.[3] Its riches are inexhaustible: "after all our diligence, to the end of our lives and to the end of the Church, it must be an unexplored and unsubdued land, with heights and valleys, forests and streams, on the right and left of our path and close about us, full of concealed wonders and choice treasures".[4] In a problem such as this, it is important to know the attitude of a man whose learning and competence in scripture and tradition are unquestionable. For he did not merely make a whole Church aware once more of the place and importance of tradition; he also succeeded in putting scripture in a new light.[5]

1. *The problem of the canon*

The demarcation of the books which belong to the Old Testament is based principally on the fact that Christ himself quoted these books and spoke of their contents. Tradition also provides pointers in this important question.[6]

The canon of the New Testament is also attested by tradition: "it is undeniable after all that we do receive the

[2] *MS* A 11, 8.

[3] *Parochial Sermons*, VI, p. 252; cf. p. 251.

[4] *Essay on Development* (2nd ed.), p. 71.

[5] Cf. L. Bouyer, *Newman*, pp. 187 f.

[6] Cf. *Tract* 85 in *Discussions*, p. 210.

New Testament in its existing shape on Tradition".[7] "The belief on which that canonicity is based has been uniform and uninterrupted in the countries which surrounded the Eastern Mediterranean and its adjacent seas, from the age of St Clement to our own".[8] Scripture itself does not inform us of its extent. It is ultimately only its history that can help us to learn the number of the books. One of Newman's sermons divides this history into eight different phases:[9]

1. The composition of various books.
2. The diffusion of these books as separate items.
3. The probable loss of some of these books.
4. The gradual collection of these books.
5. The temporary incompleteness or fluidity of this collection.
6. The reception of all by the Church in the fourth century.
7. The canon in undisturbed possession till the sixteenth century, when the Reformers rejected some.
8. The situation till the present day: Catholics believing the scripture on the authority of the Church who gives it to them; Protestants accepting some books on the authority of the Church, rejecting others on the authority of the Reformers.

[7] *Via Media*, I, p. 285; cf. *MS* D 6, 1: "We appeal to Scripture as the word of God on the authority of the Fathers".
[8] Cf. *MS* A 43, 14. Probably Clement of Alexandria (d. before 215) is meant.
[9] *MS* A 16, 4 II; appendix, no. 3.

Knowledge of the history of the canon, of how it was fixed and handed down, justifies, therefore, the Christian in accepting this canon; the authority of the Church and the content of scripture itself even oblige him to do so. But scripture as such in itself, without its history and historical setting, loses at once its external unity and cohesion. If it is not regarded as the book of the community of the Church, and if it is not clearly marked off from other books by the traditional doctrine of this same community, all the claims that are usually associated with it remain illusory.

2. The inspiration of scripture

Sacred scripture was composed by men whose will remained free and untrammelled,[10] which obviously means that the human element is fully represented in it. Such limitations are particularly evident in statements, clauses or expressions which deal with pure matters of fact where faith and morals are not involved.[11] Newman excludes such

[10] Cf. *Tract* 85 in *Discussions*, p. 146.

[11] For Newman's view of the "obiter dicta" see the detailed treatment in J. Seynaeve's excellent work, *Newman's Doctrine on Holy Scripture* pp. 169 f. The view is not contrary to the decree *Lamentabili* (especially no. 11, *Denzinger*, 2011), since Newman held the inerrancy of scripture. We can reach the same conclusion indirectly from the words of the pope under whom the decree was promulgated, when he spoke of Newman (cf. *AAS* 41, 1908, p. 200). Newman's opinion on this matter is no longer held today. See J. Schildenberger, "Inspiration und Irrtumslosigkeit der Heiligen Schrift" in Feiner, Trütsch and Böckle, ed., *Fragen der Theologie heute* (1957), pp. 100–21, especially p. 116.

elements of scripture from the influence of inspiration, calling them "obiter dicta".[12]

But scripture has also a divine author, who is in fact the principal author. He is the cause of its inspiration, and scripture is filled by the living God.[13] The Apostles and evangelists, on whom the charism of inspiration was bestowed, are the vehicles of this inspiration: whatever they write or say is inspired.[14] Since the "*verbum transmissum* is but the substance" of what an Apostle said, while the "*verbum transscriptum* is his in the very letter", scripture must be regarded as the personal work of an inspired mind, while tradition is from an inspired author only in its origin. Scripture then must be said to be inspired, but not tradition.[15] This privilege of scripture is described as follows by Newman: "Scripture has a gift which Tradition has not; it is fixed, tangible, accessible, readily applicable, and besides all this perfectly true in all its parts and relations".[16] Thus scripture approximates to a great extent to the perpetual presence of the Apostles in the Church.[17]

As regards the nature of inspiration, Newman makes a fundamental distinction between two views. The first is that each sentence was dictated by the Holy Spirit, the

[12] Cf. H. F. Davis, "Newman, the Bible and the Obiter Dicta" in *The Life of the Spirit* 8(1945), pp. 398–407.
[13] K. H. Schelkle, "Heilige Schrift und Wort Gottes" in *Theologische Quartalschrift* 138(1958), p. 259.
[14] *MS* A 16, 4 I, see appendix, no. 7 a.
[15] *MS* A 23, 1, published by J. Seynaeve, *op. cit.*, p. 121.
[16] *Via Media*, I, p 291.
[17] *Ibid.*

second that the text is in fact infallibly true.[18] "Here then are two distinct views which may be taken of inspiration; one, that it really attaches as a property to the sacred text, and to every word and letter in it";[18] the other view takes inspiration in an analogous sense, and sees scripture as the work of inspired authors.[19]

This notion of the scripture's being indirectly inspired is Newman's personal view. He knows that scripture itself has no teaching on the matter. Tradition alone can give assurance of this so essential a quality of the sacred text. But Newman is fully in accord with this tradition, as it is represented as binding in two dogmas, one, that scripture is inspired,[20] two, that the Church is its infallible interpreter.[21]

3. *The interpretation of scripture*

a) *The imperfection of its language*

Scripture contains divine truths which it expresses in human language. The disproportion between the object

---

[18] J. Seynaeve, *op. cit.*, p. 121.

[19] Cf. *Ibid.*; Seynaeve reads as follows: "Here then are two distinct views which may be taken of inspiration: one, that it really attaches as a property to the sacred text, and to carry word and letter to it", adding in a foot-note "hardly decipherable". I have given what I consider to be the correct transcription: "and to every word and letter in it".

[20] *Stray Essays*, p. 12; cf. *Denzinger*, 783, 1787.

[21] *Ibid.*; cf. Denzinger, 1788.

and the means of expressing it is at once evident. The discrepancy between the "imperfect and defective" words of scripture[22] and the perfection of its object indicates that the words of scripture mean more than they would according to ordinary human usage and estimation. They are "sacramental words".[23] They are not merely capable of explanation and interpretation, they are actually in need of it. But this interpretation is not left to the individual fancy, it demands a clear, firm directive, which is given in the tradition of the Church.

b) *The structure of scripture*

Scripture, as may be seen from the history of its origin, is not a uniform structure. It consists of a number of occasional papers: "it is not one book; it is a great number of writings, of various persons living at different times, put together into one, and assuming its existing form as if casually and by accident. It is as if you were to seize the papers or correspondence of leading men in any school of philosophy or science"[24] and hence it does not provide a system of doctrine. It was written "for those who were already instructed".[25] An author could address his readers "not with direct announcements but with intimations and

[22] *Ibid.*, p. 41: "In this point of view we may, without irreverence, speak even of the words of inspired Scripture as imperfect and defective".
[23] *Via Media*, I, p. 291; cf. J. Seynaeve, *op. cit.*, pp. 231–4.
[24] *Discussions*, p. 234. See H. Fries, *Tradition*, p. 112.
[25] *Via Media*, I, p. 158.

implications of the faith"[26] and still be understood by them. Humanly speaking, it was possible that not all doctrines were contained in scripture, but through the workings of divine providence it actually embodies the total idea of divine revelation in its intrinsic structure and in its implicit sense.[27] The result of the seemingly haphazard way in which scripture was produced is that even the intrinsic structure is unmethodical and irregular.[28] Many truths are contained in it only indirectly and implicitly.[29] Without the systematic doctrine of tradition, without its authorized interpretation and explicitation of the truths hidden beneath the surface, scripture could not be properly understood and it would remain a book full of unsolved mysteries.[30]

c) *The mystical sense*[31]

All things are present at once to the Holy Spirit, and can be expressed in his utterance, even though this is the word of man. Hence "God cannot speak without meaning many

[26] *Ibid.*

[27] Cf. *Tract* 85 in *Discussions*, pp. 150 f. This view can of course be used to justify the Anglican doctrine of the sufficiency of scripture, and the passage cited was no doubt originally meant to do so (cf. *Discussions*, p. 141, note 1). But at the same time an objective truth with regard to scripture came to light, which Newman then never gave up (cf. *Essay on Development*, 2nd ed., p. 342 etc.).

[28] *Discussions*, p. 142.

[29] *Ibid.*

[30] *Ibid.*, p. 195; cf. *Arians*, p. 51.

[31] Cf. J. Seynaeve, *op. cit.*, pp. 307–48.

things at once".[32] The word of God may be taken in its literal sense, but it may also have a "secondary sense".[33] Exegesis is pursuing an objective task when it seeks to find and justify the deeper, mystical sense. To keep exclusively to the literal sense is to construct only a partial theology, which cannot escape being heretical. The heretics of Church history practically all remained on the level of the literal sense of scripture.[34] Thus Newman can say: "It may almost be laid down as an historical fact, that the mystical interpretation and orthodoxy will stand or fall together".[35] The practice of the Fathers—except for certain exaggerations[36]—justifies completely this way of reading scripture.[37] And the authoritative interpretation given by the Church has in fact sanctioned this practice, since "all the definitions or received judgments of the early and mediaeval Church rest upon definite, even though sometimes obscure sentences of Scripture".[38]

What difference would there be between the word of God and the word of man, if the former did not possess a mysterious depth of its own? And what use would this depth be, if there were no way of fathoming it? But the

[32] *Parochial Sermons*, I, p. 271.

[33] Cf. *Arians*, p. 61; *Newman-Keble Correspondence*, p. 25: "ecclesiastical sense"; *Essay on Development* (2nd ed.), p. 346: "allegorical sense".

[34] Cf. *Essay on Development* (2nd ed.), p. 343: "the school of Antioch".

[35] *Ibid.*, p. 344.

[36] *Arians*, p. 63.

[37] *Essay on Development* (2nd ed.), pp. 339 f.

[38] *Ibid.*, p. 72.

mind of the Church is nourished and developed by means of scripture, provided that its levels of meaning are taken into account by competent interpretation.[39]

4) *Tradition as interpreter of scripture*

The result of these considerations may be summed up by saying that "the Bible does not carry with it its own interpretation".[40] But the decisive question still remains: who can give the necessary help to understanding it? The answer has already been indicated: "the testimony of past ages" is the necessary background to the understanding of scripture.[41] Then there are the systematic formulae of the creeds, and finally the decisive voice of the infallible magisterium, which as the continuation of inspiration[42] upholds the scripture and guarantees its interpretation. In other words, tradition is the necessary help to the understanding of scripture.[43]

In Newman's view, the doctrine taught by the living tradition came at the same time as scripture. God, who gave the gift of scripture, also added that of tradition.[44] "It is plain that what was generally received in the early times must have been sanctioned by the Apostles; and what the

[39] *Ibid.*, p. 339.
[40] *Via Media*, I, p. 245; cf. *Essays Critical*, I, p. 104; *Justification*, p. 118.
[41] *Essays and Sketches*, I, p. 122.
[42] Cf. *Stray Essays*, p. 13 etc.
[43] Cf. the summary of the argument in *Present Position of Catholics*, pp. 318–21.
[44] Cf. *Essays and Sketches*, I, p. 122.

Apostles ordained and taught in every Church is the best comment on what they have said in Scriptures, the fullest and truest development of those principles of faith which they have put into writing".[45] Since the essential elements of this developed doctrine delivered in the form of tradition were recorded systematically in the baptismal professions of faith and in the creeds, their role as "an additional help"[46] to understanding scripture is at once evident. But the stream of tradition can also be traced in the Fathers' testimony to the faith. In so far as they hand on the common faith, their writings and doctrine must be taken into account if the study of scripture is to be genuine and profound.[47]

Finally we have, as the infallible guardian and interpreter of scripture, the tradition of universal Church: "the Catholic Church may be said almost infallibly to interpret Scripture aright, though from the possession of past tradition".[48] The Church is in fact, as the pillar and the ground of truth, "the appointed interpreter",[49] for "when

[45] *MS* A 50, 1 (sermon no. 354, 28 August 1834), p. 29.

[46] *Parochial Sermons*, II, p. 29; cf. *Essays Critical*, II, p. 249.

[47] Cf. *Justification*, p. 121: "The Fathers as expositors of Scripture"; *Tracts Theological*, p. 200; *Lectures on Difficulties*, II, p. 64; *Miracles*, p. 373 etc.

[48] *Via Media*, I, p. 58; cf. *Essays Critical*, I, p. 163. So too K. H. Schelkle in his article "Heilige Schrift und Wort Gottes" appeals to the fellowship of the Church (pp. 267–73) as well as to scientific exegesis (pp. 262–7) for the correct interpretation of the word of God. He mentions as making up this fellowship: 1) oral tradition, 2) the organisation of the magisterium, 3) the whole living Church as a manifestation of the Spirit and its power (p. 268).

[49] *Tract* 85 in *Discussions*, p. 191.

God gave us these two means of knowledge, Scripture and Tradition, he also established an authority, to decide in cases of doubt, and gifted His Church with infallibility in her decisions regarding the knowledge of salvation".[50]

5) *Scripture as guardian of tradition*

The bearing of tradition on scripture and its influence on its interpretation must not make us lose sight of the effective role played in turn by scripture with regard to tradition. Scripture supplies a certain negative norm for tradition, which it can rightly do, since from its very nature there can be no contradiction in revelation. Just as it is certain, even theoretically, that no writings could have become canonical if they contradicted the teaching of the universal Church, so too "no tradition certainly is tenable which contradicts Scripture".[51] Scripture, therefore, has a preservative and protective function with regard to tradition: "What is written is a safeguard to what is un-written".[52] It provides proof of the doctrines put forward by tradition, which always appeals to scripture.[53]

[50] *MS* A 29, 7, p. 13.

[51] *Miracles*, p. 323.

[52] *MS* A 13, 2, "The Brothers' Controversy", *op. cit.*, p. 306, which continues: "what is unwritten is a varied comment on a (necessarily) limited text".

[53] Cf. *Via Media*, I, p. 287: "Tradition for statement, Scripture for proof" etc.

6. *The question of the sufficiency of scripture*

a) *The whole of revelation in scripture*

Newman recognized the pre-eminent position of scripture, as has already been emphasized.[54] As an Anglican, following the sixth of the Thirty-nine Articles, he held that it was the only source of truths binding in faith. He held, therefore, that the whole of revelation was contained in scripture, a view for which he found abundant confirmation in the Fathers.[55]

When Newman came to discuss the doctrine of the Council of Trent, the work of his learned friend, William Palmer, was of considerable help to him. In his famous *Treatise on the Church of Christ* Palmer had said of the Fathers of the Council of Trent: "They did not venture to affirm . . . that the Christian verity was contained partly in written books, and partly in unwritten traditions".[56]

---

[54] Cf. e.g. *Parochial Sermons*, I, pp. 158, 219, 225, 248, 307 etc.

[55] Cf. *Via Media*, I, p. 315; *MS* D 6, 1, Letter II, p. 26, where Newman quotes the following Fathers for the sufficiency of scripture: St Vincent of Lerins, Tertullian, Origen, St Optatus, St Basil the Great, St Augustine, St John Chrysostom, Anastasius of Antioch, St Athanasius, St Cyrill of Jerusalem and Theodoret.

[56] W. Palmer, *Treatise on the Church of Christ* (1838), II, p. 15, quoted in *Essay on Development* (2nd ed.), p. 339, note 1. On the whole question, see J. R. Geiselmann, "Die Tradition" in *Fragen der Theologie heute*, pp. 69–108, and especially his "Das Konzil von Trient über das Verhältnis der Heiligen Schrift und der nicht geschriebenen Traditionen" in *Die mündliche Überlieferung, op. cit.*, pp. 123–206.

Understood in this way, the declaration of Trent, that revelation was contained "in the written books *and* in the unwritten traditions",[57] could not provide an occasion for giving up the doctrine of the sufficiency of scripture. As a Catholic, Newman could safely hold, without misgivings, that the whole Christian faith was contained in scripture. He found enough support for this view among Catholics to assure him that it was correct, and he could appeal to the ancient and constant use of the "mystical sense" by Fathers and theologians, since it was invoked to give a scriptural foundation to all the Catholic doctrines. And he saw no change in later theology: "Nor am I aware that later post-Tridentine writers deny that the whole Catholic faith may be proved from scripture, though they would certainly maintain that it is not to be found on the surface of it".[58] If, as an Anglican, he accepted the maxim that all truths necessary to salvation were to be found in scripture,[59] as a Catholic he could affirm that the whole of revelation was, in a certain sense, contained in scripture.[60]

Newman had no great difficulty in maintaining his original view uninterruptedly and without change. He did not, and never had, understood the doctrine of the sufficiency of scripture in the Protestant sense of *sola scriptura*.

[57] Cf. *Denzinger*, 783; J. Ranft, *Ursprung*, pp. 5 f.
[58] Cf. *Essay on Development*, p. 342; here he names, as upholders of the view that all truth must be derived from scripture: St Ignatius of Antioch, St Polycarp, St Irenaeus, St Cyprian, St Alphonsus Liguori, Salmeron, Cornelius a Lapide and others.
[59] *Jager*, p. 380; *Essays and Sketches*, III, p. 114; *Via Media*, I, pp. 284, 292.
[60] *Lectures on Difficulties*, II, pp. 11 f.

Even according to Anglican doctrine, he had always taken tradition to be a necessary "source of information"[61] and of interpretation, though in a subordinate role.

Thus the formula, "all revelation in Scripture", reflects a very definite basic view in Newman's theology, which is voiced in his notion of scripture as such as well as in his attitude to Christian doctrine as a whole. It is enough for any doctrine, that at least "one view of the mystery" in question be found in scripture.[62] With regard to scripture, it is enough that the doctrine can be found beneath the surface, at least in the wider and mystical sense of scripture.[63] On this basis Newman holds that the doctrine of the sufficiency of scripture is valid for the truths of Christian revelation.

b) *Living tradition in relation to scripture*

When dealing with this problem in his investigation of Newman's doctrine of inspiration, J. Seynaeve came to the conclusion that "while as an Anglican he denied the authority of tradition, he virtually admitted it".[64] Otto Karrer, on the other hand, when he takes up the theme in

---

[61] *Via Media*, I, p. 28; cf. *Mozley*, II, p. 113 and the address to the Bible Society in J. Seynaeve, *op. cit.*, p. 12.

[62] *Fifteen Sermons*, p. 336: "whether that one view of the mystery of which all such are the exponents, be not there".

[63] Cf. *Discussions*, p. 141; *Essay on Development*, p. 342.

[64] J. Seynaeve, *op. cit.*, pp. 44 f.

his discussion with Asmussen, says that according to Newman "the whole of revelation is contained in scripture, even though only more or less explicitly".[65] The two writers indicate the starting-points which give rise to the problem. According to Newman, revelation is a great and fertile "idea", some aspects of which have been made explicit, while others have still to be unfolded. These aspects are presented and preserved in scripture and in tradition, in written or oral form, as the case may be. To present the whole idea adequately is only possible to a limited extent, by the nature of human speech and writing. But at the same time, it is enough to have grasped correctly even a portion, in order to possess the whole system in a certain fashion.[66] Thus scripture may preserve more details and transmit them with more literal exactness than tradition. Still, it contains no more than the whole in the details. And tradition, less rich in particulars, also contains the whole, though in another form and under other aspects: as a "system" and a "philosophy" it has virtualities which substantiate the whole of revelation contained in scripture.

To do justice to Newman's view, therefore, we must formulate it as follows: scripture contains particulars which were not taken over by tradition, and tradition contains truths which do not lie on the surface of scripture. Thus with regard to the expression and formulation, the outward presentation, revelation may be said to be found

[65] Asmussen-Karrer, *Trennung und Einigung im Glauben*, pp. 48 f.
[66] Cf. *Gregorianum* 39 (1958), p. 594; *Discourses*, p. 344.

"partly" in each of two sources, and to this extent and from this point of view, the "*partim*" of the debates of Trent can still be justified.[67] But from the point of view of the content, that is, as regards the doctrine and the substance, the sufficiency of scripture must be affirmed, since it represents the whole of revelation, presented with a multitude of detail. So too in Newman's mind the sufficiency of tradition must be maintained, since he saw it as the life of the universal Church throughout the ages, which bears within it the whole of revelation and hands it down faithfully.[68]

[67] Cf. J. R. Geiselmann, *Überlieferung nach dem Konzil von Trient*, p. 237 etc.

[68] Cf. G. Biemer, "Die doppelte Suffizienz der Glaubensquellen und ihre Bedeutung nach Kardinal Newman" in *Theologische Quartalschrift* 140 (1960), pp. 385–409.

Conclusion

STRONG CONTROVERSY grew up about the concept of tradition or traditions after Trent,[1] and the discussion has not died down to the present day. That it was carried on vigorously in the nineteenth century is proved by the fruitful contribution made to it by Newman.

It is, however, not easy to define which of the many meanings of tradition occur at any given point in Newman's writings. As an Anglican and as a Catholic, he often used the word in a wide, non-theological sense. Tradition or traditions can be historical[2] with reference to general or to Church history,[3] they can be cultural,[4] juridical and

[1] Cf. J. R. Geiselmann, *op. cit.*, p. 135 etc.

[2] *Lectures on Difficulties*, II, pp. 262, 273; *Catholic Sermons*, p. 122; *Essays and Sketches*, III, p. 229.

[3] *Lectures on Difficulties*, II, p. 193; *Catholic Sermons*, p. 118.

[4] *Occasional Sermons*, p. 204; *Lectures on Difficulties*, I, p. 303; *Grammar of Assent*, p. 274.

political,[5] they can designate legendary[6] or inauthentic traits.[7] Thus there can be "secret",[8] "broken",[9] "mythical",[10] "human"[11] and divine traditions, "unauthorized"[12] and authorized traditions.

And then finally there is the specifically theological tradition, the subject of this book, a tradition which again displays a rich variety of forms. It can be taken in a broad sense, as the tradition of the records of the faith in general, or in a narrower sense, as oral tradition, which again can be dogmatic or liturgical. But this distinction is only an aid to surveying the wide range of differences which the forms of tradition present.

The difficulties of which we speak are due to some extent to the many dimensions to which the concept of tradition may be extended. To understand all its bearings in Newman, it is necessary to recall some characteristic features of his way of thinking.

First of all, the historical fact of Newman's Anglican origins must be taken into account. His original terminology was marked by the views laid down in Anglican

[5] *Lectures on Difficulties*, I, pp. 155 f.; *Discourses*, p. 242.

[6] *MS* A 33, 1: "according to tradition she was brought into the temple", "this vow of virginity made according to tradition"; *Lectures on Difficulties*, II, p. 57; *Essay on Development*, p. 347; *Fifteen Sermons*, p. 342; *Parochial Sermons*, VIII, p. 125; II, p. 4.

[7] *Miracles*, pp. 117 f., 268.

[8] *Essays and Sketches*, III, pp. 294, 334: "secret tradition".

[9] *Parochial Sermons*, VII, p. 119: "broken traditions".

[10] *Grammar of Assent*, p. 261.

[11] *Essays Critical*, II, p. 361; *Grammar of Assent*, p. 246.

[12] *Present Position of Catholics*, p. 45.

theology, which could not but affect the problem of tradition in particular. Then there is the well-known fact that Newman did not as a rule propound his theology in technical terms.[18] At the beginning of the theological studies which he undertook in Rome, he took great pains to master scholastic terminology, and Perrone tried to bring Newman's very personal way of expressing himself into line with the language of the schools. But Newman could never fully adapt his way of thinking to this nomenclature. Writings like the *Essay on Development* and the *Grammar of Assent* can only be comprised in scholastic categories to a very limited extent. So too the considerations on tradition in the letter to Father Flanagan and in the manuscript *On Church* are marked by the special traits of the original thinker, who is producing and using his own forms of expression. That we have here the ancient truths in a new dress for a new age, we need not doubt. For Newman, loyalty to tradition lay at the heart of his theological thinking.

A third difficulty arises when one investigates the teaching of Newman and his notion of tradition in particular. Practically all of his writings were produced as the occasion demanded, and they followed no systematic purpose. Such "occasional" writings, containing perhaps incidental references to this theme or that which could, for instance, appear as part of a sermon preached for an historical occasion, can, in the nature of things, hardly present a theological system.

---

[18] Cf. H. F. Davis in *Blackfriars* (1958), p. 310: "a notoriously untechnical writer".

Hence it is very difficult, and sometimes not quite feasible, to give a clear and consistent picture of his various statements on a given theme, uttered as they were at different times and couched in varying terms. It is not easy to decide what is provisional and what is final, and when one can or must replace views which he abandoned by new ones which he arrived at later. Finally, it must be noted that his way of expressing himself varies according to the end in view: the language of his sermons differs from that of his essays, that of his polemical writings from that of his personal letters.

In spite of all these difficulties, it must be affirmed that Newman always renders his thought clearly and cautiously, and for the most part even trenchantly, with a constant regard to fundamentals. It was one of the marks of his undoubted genius that the basic structure of this thought and the co-ordination with the whole can be observed in all his assertions. He succeeds in making the most out-of-the-way situations become tributary to his central and definitive thought.

At the end of our examination of his doctrine on tradition it can be affirmed that his thought follows a continuous and consistent line, from its first principles, through every assault and counter-assault, to the final consequences and affirmations.

Newman's contribution to the doctrine of tradition has been tentatively presented in these pages, but its work is not finished. It must be engrafted into the great structure of Catholic theology, so that it can flourish and be fruitful, since "growth is the only proof of life".

APPENDIX

Manuscripts of Newman, dealing with Tradition, from the Newman Archives in the Oratory, Birmingham

1

. . . that the duty of God's servant was to heed them[2] not, but to keep to what is old, waiting for their God and Saviour from heaven.

St Paul says that we are to "give more earnest heed to the things which we have heard" (Heb 2:1). By "things which we have heard" he seems to mean the gospel system once delivered. He does not speak here of the Creed merely, or the Commandments, or the rites and ordinances of the Church, but of that *one* system which Christ and his

[1] *MS* A 50, 4, sermon no. 474.
[2] i.e. "novelties and changes".

Apostles had given. In another passage of his epistle, he mentions one or two of the elementary facts of this system, but at the same time expressly says that he does not confine his remarks to them. He says he would have his brothers to whom he writes "go on to perfection". These elements, however, of the gospel which he mentions, serve to show us the nature of the religious system which in the text he commands to his brethren's care. They are these, "repentance, faith, baptism, laying on of hands, the resurrection, and the eternal judgment" (Heb 6).—The system built upon this beginning was to be faithfully retained as a whole . . .

2

SERMON OUTLINE, 10 JULY, 1849[3]

On Tradition

1. Meaning of the word—unwritten Tradition.

2. All bodies must have (1) things beyond writing (Houses of Parliament), (2) apparently clashing with them— —custom.

3. Common law   a stream goes silently   till an obstacle shows its strength.   a dispute or controversy brings out a point as a lawsuit showing where the right lies   Blackstone on common law[4]   Law is quite a

---

[3] *MS* A 16, 4 II, loose leaf.
[4] W. Blackstone, *Commentaries on the Law of England*, 4 vols. (1769).

case in point   points being determined   History not noticing things till they come in its way. N.B. On inspiration not in 39 articles.

4. Christianity of New Testament.   [5]nothing written at first.

> (3) [6]Scripture was not written at first
> (1) go teach—Acts   "teaching much people"
> (2) "what I delivered to you"—traditions, authority, word, etc. "customs translated instead of [7]traditions"

5. How error prevented

> 1. Union of Churches in Christianity. "We have no such customs neither the Churches of God".
> 2. Infallibility

5*. Heresies bringing out doctrine—Doctrine
> new . . . 11[8] implicit and explicit . . .

6.   Tradition of the Pharisees—put it first as an objection this text—then retort it on Protestants—say this is not meant as a mere sharp argu(men)t, but as a deep truth. they think no other interpretation good but that which

---

[5] The word omitted here is illegible. Nearly all the sermon outlines are difficult to verify, being written hastily and only key-words being used. There are numerous corrections and abbreviations.

[6] Newman indicates on the MS that this line is to go here.

[7] Reading uncertain.

[8] As the page is torn at the bottom, nothing can be read here.

they are used to. they fancy they go by private judgment but they are slaves of a tradition.

3

SERMON OUTLINE, 10 JULY, 1849[9]

On Scripture.

1. Protestants speak much about the Bible, the whole Bible etc. Bible Society. "the word of God"—against the "Apocrypha".

2. This with two reasons:
    1. Catholics correcting and corrupting the Bible
    2. that the Bible is ag(ain)st them

3. What Catholics on the other hand say is this: they agree with Protestants that the Bible is inspired—
    (1) that the Bible is only part of the word of God—(2) that the "Apocrypha" is part of the Bible—(3) that reading the Bible is not necessary to salvation

4. historical[10]   of the canon
    (1) writing of separate books
    (2) circulated separately Luke IV, Acts VIII

---

[9] *MS* A 16, 4 II. On a loose leaf along with the outline of the sermon "On Tradition". The leaf (25.6 by 20.3 cm) was folded once and inserted under the last page of the book of sermons (*MS* A 16, 4II).
[10] The missing word is illegible; perhaps "case".

(3) some perhaps lost—Col IV, Epistle to the Leodiceans

(4) gradually collected together

(5) not all received everywhere   instances Heb, Apocalypse.   St Jerome receiving only Hebrew of Old Testament[11]

(6) Church receiving in 4th century all

(7) So till Reformation; then Reformation cast out few[12] of the books

(8) So it has come down to Caths and Prots—Catholics believed the Scripture because the Church gives it them—Protestants partly because the Church . . .,[13] and partly because Reformers put some books out.

5. Protestants—In either case they believe that Scripture is God's book on the word of man. They talk much of believing in the word of God, not of course[14], but who but man taught them that Scripture is the word of God? who put the books of Scripture together? the Church—then they believe on the word of the Church—who cast out what they call the Apocrypha?—the Reformers—therefore they refrain from believing certain books on the word of the Reformers.

[11] i.e. only the Hebrew part of the Old Testament.

[12] Reading uncertain.

[13] Illegible.

[14] Reading uncertain.

Why do they believe the Reformers ?

Why do they believe the Church, yet talk ag(ain)st it?

6. On the other hand, the Catholics . . .[15] they believe both Scripture and Tradition as they would believe an Apostle or Prophet.

6. [16]On objection that the Bible is ag(ain)st the teaching of the Church—.[17]

Obj. You have stories of those who read the Bible becoming Protestants—true—but they are Protestants *before* they begin to read—and they read in disobedience— they don't need the Bible to make them Protestants.

On the other hand, I have known various Protestants who have been drawn to Catholicity by reading the Bible. But I fully believe the more we read the Bible the better Protestants[18] shall we be.   how can it be otherwise if both Church and Bible come from one author.

I wish Catholics read the Bible more. In this country where there is so much reading, it w(oul)d be a great blessing to them. It is what is the [19]remaining life of Protestants that they enjoy this gift, though in a heretical translation. It is a comfort to think how many Protestants

---

[15] Scarcely legible; probable reading: "quite consistent".

[16] 7th section marked 6th in error by Newman.

[17] Illegible.

[18] The context demands that this should be "Catholics".

[19] Illegible.

in invincible ignorance, have through God's mercy gained
spiritual good from the Bible without Church etc.[20]

4

EXCERPTS FROM THE MS "ON CHURCH"[21]

Coetus cui traditur veritas (Rom 3:2)

homines quibus traditur   creditur

Objection. No body to which veritas traditur—com-
         mendatur littera scripturae

Answers 1. the littera scripta says the contrary Rom X,
            Acts VIII, Is XXX

        2. especially the parallel to the law.[22] whether
           the letter did not preclude a judge—Vid. "A
           prophet shall see" and "The priest's lips keep
           knowledge"

        3. Fathers aga(in)st it from the first

        4. Experience shows it is nugatory.

If there be a revelation its subject (matter) must be true
. . . and its mode infallible.

This infallible revelation of truth once for all given must
be made by inspiration. either

1. directly to the (each) soul—as quakers and mystics say

---

[20] Cf. *Parochial Sermons*, VI, p. 171: "the possession of the Holy Scripture is an inestimable gift in a country to those who use it rightly".
[21] *MS* A 18, 20.   [22] Illegible.

2. at intervals or in a succession—as no one says except Mahometans

3. once for all; as is the case, viz. through inspired Apostles. It was in the beginning by inspiration, but not since. The question is, what is the revelation now that the inspired Apostles are withdrawn—
either 1. their actual work—(as the tables of the law)—
   an autograph—a temple etc. which no one thinks
   or 2. some memory of their work—i.e. their work
   carried on by the instrumentality of others
   or   in the sense or other tradition

Traditio then now is the revelatio; i.e. its matter is true and infallible.

Traditio is either

1. a locutio—oral tradition—as catechizing vid. the case of St. Anthony, Didymus, and the barbarians St. Irenaeus speaks of.

2. symbola and commandments[23] as the Mass[24]
or 2. a scriptio
   if a scriptio either—a transcriptio (translation) of the
   writings of the Apostles—a statement or record of
   their savings or writings
or 3. both

[23] Reading uncertain.
[24] The whole line was added afterwards in pencil. Hence the double enumeration.

It consists in both (vid. reason for it overleaf A)[25]—i.e. in oral tradition, in transcription (of inspired writings), and in statements or records—and not separately only but mixed—e.g. oral trad(itio)n and statements together, or in statements and transcription together. or oral, statements, and transcription etc.

But[26] now, as being virtually the revelation, it must be infallible.

The next question is who are the organs of this infallible Tradition? in some way or other, men.

If so—either 1. inspired—disproved above—if inspired not
    a tradition but a revelatio.
      2. coetus i.e. a Church.

Therefore the definition of the Church is, coetus revelans verbum Dei, or coetus cui traditur verbum revelatum ut ab eo praedicetur (this agrees with Perrone) or coetus tradentium verbum revelatum, or coetus praedicantium.

And its forma is Praedicatio or Traditio Verbi

And (from what has been said above) is[27] gift or qualification, is infallibilitas i.e. *in sua materia*, i.e. in verbo revelato. N.B. It is also a coetus credentium, but this as individuals. It is like the distinction between docens and discens.

[25] This reference cannot be verified.
[26] Illegible. The text perhaps reads "But anyhow . . ."
[27] Probably "its".

5

Infallibility of the Church in teaching doctrine whether in faith or in morals

She is 1. sufficient for herself as everything which has life—self-conservation.

2. knows her depositum ⎫ by a divine assisten-
3. knows its boundaries ⎭   tia

4. will never be allowed to say that that is revealed which is not, nor that that is not, which is.

The great
maxim is
"Securus
judicat
orbis . . ."

5. or to act in any way by word or deed which is prejudiced to the depositum, which is not necessary or useful to it.

6. She knows what opinions are agreeable or serviceable and what are contrary and hurtful to the depositum.

[28] *MS* B 7, 4.

7. She cannot, from the nature of the case, increase its depositum.

(N.B. . . . The main point I wish to ascertain is, whether I may not hold

1. The Church's infallibility is *wholly* ministrative to the depositum (Custos, testis, judex, magistra) . . . and does not exist except as far as she is custos, testis, judex, magistra depositi.

2. That none of her assertions must be received under pain of damnation, except such as are declarative and definitive of the depositum).[29]

When we say that the Church's infallibility protects herself, this means when regarded as a whole and when she does so on principle. It need not be so as regards particular, undeliberate and local acts. If, as now, she lays down by the mouth of her chief Pastor with the assent of a great number of Bishops, that the temporal power is at present necessary for the spiritual,[30] we may well believe that she is stating a *providential* fact, which it would be wrong to doubt. But this would not necessarily apply to such acts as the conduct of Paul III or Pius IV towards England; nor again to the conduct of Vigilius, Honorius, John XXII, etc.

---

[29] To understand Newman's point here, it must be remembered that this was before the First Vatican Council.
[30] See for instance the official pronouncements of Pius IX on the defence of the Papal States.

6

SERMON ON THE HOLY SPIRIT[31]

Our Lord said many things to them which they could not understand, and He had many things to say. 'I have many things to say to you but you cannot bear them'.

Our Lord had spoken, it seems to me, many words to the Apostles in parables and other ways. Not only those recorded in Scripture.

He spoke very many words which are not written there which have come down to us by what is called tradition. So the word of God is written and unwritten.

There is a great part in the Gospels,   still He said a great deal to them which is not written and never has been only by chance now and then.

St Paul in the Acts of the Apostles tells things not in the Gospels so that He said a great many gracious things which are not in the Gospels.

---

[31] The sermon is preserved in fragmentary state in a transcription which has the following note in pencil: "These are fragments of a sermon preached by Dr. Newman (date not given). The history of them is this. Mr Maher engaged a reporter, Mr Hackney, on his own account. Mr Hackney having made the notes delivered them when service was over at Mr Maher's house. Mr Maher had entirely lost these and other sermon notes—but these were afterwards found by Miss Maher among some music and given by her to me in the short hand.—Mr Hackney in this month April 1875 wrote them out as best he could sending me word that at the distance of so many years he could not easily and in part not at all decipher his writing and had therefore left gaps. Moreover some portions had been torn out".

They were often hard sayings still they treasured them so that they have remained in the Church and these are great truths which the Holy Ghost has to bring out and make more plain   so that the Holy Ghost is ever present in the Church   and in a certain sense.

They are the words 'I have many things yet to say to you but you cannot bear them now'.

Those are the things they could not understand.

Sometimes, you know, the Apostles asked Him what He meant.

The Holy Ghost explains these things to the Church to the end of time.

'When the Spirit of truth shall come He will teach you all the truth'. That does not mean that He will begin a new revelation, He will explain that which was given.

God has given many revelations—to Adam—to Noah—to Abraham—to the Jews—to the Prophets.

He has given a number of new revelations which never were in the world before.

The Holy Ghost would explain not new but old truths. In the first place truth is shown to us by the representatives of Christ and the Apostles."

There is a further transcription of the same sermon:[32]

"Our Lord had spoken, it seems to me, many words to the Apostles in parables . . . Not only those recorded in Scripture. He spoke very many words which are not written there which have come down to us by what is called tradition, so the word of God is written and unwrit-

[32] *MS* A 33, 1.

183

ten. There is a great part in the Gospels, still He said a great deal to them which is not written and never has been only by chance now and then. Paul in the Acts of the Apostles tells things not in the Gospels so that He said a great many gracious things which are not in the Gospels. They were often hard sayings still they treasured them so that they have remained in the Church and these are the great truths which the Holy Ghost has to bring out and make more and more plain, so that the Holy Ghost is ever present in the Church and in a certain sense they are the words 'I have many things yet to say to you, but you cannot bear them now' . . . The Holy Ghost explains these things to the Church to the end of time.

7

SERMON FOR 11TH SUNDAY AFTER PENTECOST, 9 AUGUST, 1874

a) Sermon outline[33]

Intro(duction) Revelation—Word of God   Recapitulation.

Scripture—Scriptures—2 Testaments   Bible, treachery and therefore Inspiration:

1. What I say "inspired", and not in science, or art etc.
2. Difference of Old and New. Old imperfect and through so many ages. New perfect and once for all in one age (Heb 1:1). Here I speak of the New.

[33] *MS* A 16, 4 I, p. 170 (verso).

3. The Apostle—inspired—Our Lord, God.
4. Objection: Why not their words, of their writings? not their speeches? why not their conversation? of course it was. All they said about religion was. They might not know about the earth going round the sun etc.
5. but it may be objected on the other hand that such sayings were not recollected.—but some might be.
6. This is what Catholics call "tradition"—and in which we differ from Protestants. Meaning of the word "tradition". Vide Epistle for this Sunday[34].
7. Things we know by tradition.

For this
Protestants
need tradition.

1. That Scripture is inspired word of God.
2. what books the Bible consists of
3. the mass etc. etc.

8. And so natural(ly) every school, every set of workmen[35] go by Trad(itio)n— "common law" is tradition.
9. Hence we say there are two parts of the word of God, written and unwritten.
10. But still surely tradition may go wrong. Yes, and Scripture may be wrongly interpreted—
11. Therefore, the Church decides as being infallible.

[34] I Cor 15:1–10.
[35] Reading uncertain.

12. Hence there may be mistaken reports of miracles, prophecies etc.—but we must see what the *Church* says about them.

b) Fragment of hearer's notes of this sermon of 9 August, 1874[36]

This I said last week—and then I spoke of the Old Testament. Now what more concerns us the New. made up—immediate Apostles and disciples of our Lord from the first writing to the last   disclosed more and more   in the Old Testament not in   for our Lord made a perfect revelation of his will, a record of which we have in the New. In the New it is revealed in one generation   Then He spoke Himself   it is our book of reading inspired

When I say that it comes from God to teach us to go to heaven   St Paul has said "not many . . ."   In the Old King Solomon   The wisest of men—knowledge about birds, beasts, fishes, flowers   but he fell away we don't know whether he is saved   So it was in spite of   not one single step to heaven   but what his mind was able When I say Scripture is inspired   I don't mean to say things of this earth   at the time our Lord came on earth   Supposing they are right it does not prove that the Apostles knew with   they spoke of what related to Heaven—their knowledge was knowledge unto salva-

---

[36] *MS* C 5, 1.—The manuscript is marked "Words written down at the time of sermon . . ."

tion   St Peter says, "All Scripture . . ."   but divine
truth   to reprove correct   teach them how to please
God   all has reference   teaches us where to go for
grace   not of this world we shall be for ever in the
state in which we die   better to have   than all the
knowledge of King Solomon   "Vanity of Vanities"
Now a question may be asked   If they thus had revealed
to them   the truth of eternity   of course   when
they spoke as well as when they wrote

   Of the contradiction[37] in their words   what they
said   If St Paul made a speech it is (not)[38] probable he was
not inspired   not contradiction   Then it may be said
     why do we go by writers   not said   The whole
time of the Apostles was taken up in questions   they spoke
more than they wrote   Why is only what is written to
be considered as   revelation and not   Protestants
make a keen distinction   because they[39]. between
great advantage in writing   It is not true   That is
what we call Tradition   i.e. what has come down from
the Apostles   yet not written by them   Tradition is a
handing down   from mouth to mouth from father to
son   When a priest catechizes   In the Epistle of
today we have a clear instance of this Tradition   what
we convey to children in the catechism   the Bible not
known   converts made before the New Testament was
written   This the way he speaks   "I make known"

[37] Reading uncertain.

[38] This insertion seems to be necessary for the sense.

[39] Illegible.

He speaks of the time when he only preached   these
what we call the *Creed*   as truth not written came down
from the Apostles   That is called Tradition   The
written Scripture unwritten Tradition   We shall find
there are many things we   have knowledge of from
tradition   instance   the Bible   inspired how do
we that by Tradition   The books that are inspired
and Protestants who disclaim Tradition   The rites and
ceremonies of Holy Mass   It is most astonishing
books of the Fathers because conveyed down to them here
is the very same   It is said the Holy Mass   4 or 500
years and when we come to consider that is the very way
that goes on at present one company of men   many
rules not written   a school tradition[40].   of things
the Headmaster if he attempt to go against those rules
w(oul)d find it most difficult   a still more remarkable
instance in law   statute laws
Parliament   after all a law still higher   common
law   no written law making death for murder   the
reason being by Tradition   always consider not written
has more strength   in Government we go by tradition
Therefore when it is so determined   by Catholics
that there is an unwritten law as well as a written
profession   therefore unnatural to say the   Tradition
is not   You may say how can we know what comes
from God? errors   natural   but easy answered
We have that which the world has not
God knows the heart of man the danger wrongly

[40] Illegible

interpreted   Greek Hebrew its sense perhaps obscure
     how are we to be sure of the right sense?   how
are we to be sure we have the right tradition?

Many parts we can prove to have come down from the
Apostles
     The   when God gave these to man   knowledge
     The Church the gift of *infallibility*   which always
determines   I never saw such an   The Church in
(most important)[41] cases has Divine   quite lately   St.
Matthew "Blessed art thou Simon . . . rock"   Now you
know that text explains

In the last four years   the Vatican   the Bishops
determined   as being collected in one   they determined from that text   that the Pope was the expounder
of   Many stories have come down   legends   not
the whole have been pronounced as true   The rites of
the Mass   God has pronounced by the Church   they
do come from the Apostles   We must see in what the
Church has decided   Perhaps in another century   till
then open   all important things are decided by Holy
Church already   We ought to thank God we are not
left to decide for ourselves   Protestant   Bible
Said to have happened   miracles   prophecies   Yet
Holy Church has said   Let us thank God we are not
left with a half revelation to float on the world as it were
     but has continued the line of the Apostles   Say
Lord   The Holy Ghost answers those questions   We
must pray for our   This country of England   If only

[41] This part is in pencil in the manuscript, which shows the uncer-
tainty of the writer.

189

this great country accepted   not to wander on the earth.

c) Excerpts of later notes of this sermon of 9 August, 1874[42]

If the Apostles were inspired when they wrote, and had the truths so clearly revealed to them, was their speaking not inspired as well? If not, their words might have contradicted their writings, all their teaching might have been a contradiction to themselves. Then it might be said: Why do we go by what the Apostles wrote and not by what they said? Their whole time was taken up in teaching, they spoke a great deal more than they wrote. Protestants will receive as the word of God only what the Apostles wrote, not what they spoke, because they reject Tradition. By Tradition we mean this: giving over from mouth to mouth as it were—from father to son[43], what the Apostles spoke! Their teaching was like our catechism and we are to teach now what they taught.

Surely there are great advantages in writing; what is written can be handed over unchanged from generation to

[42] *MS* A 29, 7.—The manuscript is marked: "written down from memory by a pupil teacher".
[43] Cf. *MS* A 33, 1, where exactly the same formulations are found. This undated manuscript seems to be another transcription of Newman's sermon of 9 August 1874. But it may simply be a copy of one of the previous transcriptions, especially as there are no new expressions to prove the originality of this manuscript.

generation, and forms a steady basis to teaching by mouth.

Tradition makes customs pass into law.

. . . when God gave us these two means of knowledge: Scripture and Tradition, he also established an authority, to decide in cases of doubt, and gifted His Church with infallibility in her decisions regarding the knowledge of salvation . . .

When a text of Scripture admits of different interpretations as long as the Church does not decide about its sense, the question remains open, that means we may believe about it what we please.

The same is the case with many traditions, with the legends that are current, reports of wonderful cures, apparitions etc; as long as the Church has not pronounced upon them, we are free to reject or admit them . . .

A living expounder of the truth was needed, and God gave it in the Church through which the Holy Ghost answers those questions which arise from time to time.[44]

[44]This manuscript contains a note in Newman's own handwriting: "Clear and good".

SELECT BIBLIOGRAPHY

I. Sources

THE STANDARD edition of the collected works of Newman is that of Longmans, Green and Co., London (1874–1921), in 40 volumes. A complete survey of his works is given by A. Läpple in H. Fries and W. Becker, ed., *Kardinal–Newman–Studien* (1948–57), vol. I, pp. 287–94. Cf. the supplements to this survey given by N. Schiffer and W. Becker in vol. II, p. 325, and by W. Becker and G. Biemer in vol. III, pp. 286–92.

a) The works of John Henry Cardinal Newman in chronological order

Note: Whenever two dates of publication are cited below, quotations in the text of this book have been taken from the second edition, except where stated otherwise.

Two Essays on Biblical and on Ecclesiastical Miracles (1842–3; 1870).
The Arians of the Fourth Century (1833).
Tracts for the Times, 5 vols. (1833–40).
Parochial and Plain Sermons, 8 vols. (1834–43).
"The Brothers' Controversy" in *British Critic* 39 (1836), pp. 166–99.

The Via Media of the Anglican Church: vol. I. *Lectures on the Prophetical Office of the Church. Viewed Relatively to Romanism and Popular Protestantism* (1837); vol. II. *Occasional Letters and Tracts* (1891).

Lectures on the Doctrine of Justification (1838).

Sermons Bearing on Subjects of the Day (1843; 1869).

Fifteen Sermons preached before the University of Oxford (1843; 1872).

An Essay on the Development of Christian Doctrine (1845; 1878).

Loss and Gain. The Story of a Convert (1848; 1893).

Discourses Addressed to Mixed Congregations (1849).

Lectures on Certain Difficulties Felt by Anglicans in Catholic Teaching: vol. I. *Twelve Lectures Addressed to the Anglican Party of* 1833 (1850), vol II. *A Letter Addressed to the Rev. E. B. Pusey, D. D., on Occasion of his Eirenicon of* 1864.—*A Letter Addressed to His Grace the Duke of Norfolk on Occasion of Mr. Gladstone's Recent Expostulation of* 1874 (1875).

Lectures on the Present Position of Catholics in England (1851).

The Idea of a University Defined and Illustrated (1852; 1873).

Sermons Preached on Various Occasions (1857).

The Office of the Holy Ghost under the Gospel (1857).

"On Consulting the Faithful in Matters of Doctrine", in *The Rambler* (1859), pp. 198–230; edited with an introduction by J. Coulson (1961).

Apologia pro Vita Sua, Being a History of His Religious Opinions (1864; 1865).

Verses on Various Occasions (1867).

An Essay in Aid of a Grammar of Assent (1870).

Essays Critical and Historical, 2 vols. (1871).

Tracts Theological and Ecclesiastical (1871; 1872).

Historical Sketches, 3 vols. (1872).

Discussions and Arguments on Various Subjects (1872).

The Development of Religious Error (1885).

Stray Essays, Essays on Controversial Points Variously Illustrated (1890, privately).

Le Protestantisme aux Prises avec la Doctrine Catholique. Correspondance avec deux Ministres Anglais, by Jean-Nicolas Jager (2nd edition, 1836).

Letters and Correspondence of John Henry Newman during his Life in the Anglican Church, 2 vols., ed. by Anne Mozley (1891).

Meditations and Devotions (1893).

Addresses to Cardinal Newman with his Replies etc., 1879–81, ed. by W. P. Neville (1905).

Sermon Notes of John Henry Cardinal Newman, 1849–78, ed. by Fathers of the Birmingham Oratory (1913).

Correspondence of John Henry Newman with John Keble and others, 1839–45, ed. by Fathers of the Birmingham Oratory (1917).

Newman—Perrone Paper on Development, ed. by T. Lynch, in *Gregorianum* 14 (1935), pp. 402–7.

Essays and Sketches, 3 vols., ed. by Ch. Fr. Harrold (1948).

"Newman Manuscripts on Holy Scripture", ed. by Jaak Seynaeve, in *Cardinal Newman's Doctrine on Holy Scripture according to his Published Works and Previously Unedited Manuscripts*, Appendix 1—150 (1953).

Autobiographical Writings, ed. by Henry Tristram of the Oratory (1956).

Catholic Sermons of Cardinal Newman. Published for the First Time, from the Cardinal's Autograph Manuscripts, ed. by Fathers of the Birmingham Oratory (1957).

"An Unpublished Paper by Cardinal Newman on the Development of Doctrine", ed. by H. M. Achával, S.J., in *Gregorianum* 39 (1958), pp. 585–96.—C. S. Dessain in *JTS*, new series 9 (October, 1958), pp. 324–35.

Previously unpublished manuscripts of Newman and transcriptions of sermons in the appendix.

b) Works of Anglican theologians, 16th to 19th Century

Barrow, Isaac (1630–77), *Works* I—VIII (3rd edition, 1830).

Beveridge, William (1637–1701), *Works* I–XII (Oxford, 1848).

Bramhall, John (1594–1663), *Works* I–V (1845).

Bull, George (1634–1710), *Works* I–VI (1827).

Burnet, Gilbert (1643–1715), *An Exposition of the Thirty-nine Articles of the Church of England* (1831).

Butler, Joseph (1692–1752), *The Analogy of Religion, Natural and Revealed, to the Constitution and Course of Nature* (1871).

Butler, William Archer (1814–48), *Letters on the Development of Christian Doctrine in Reply to Mr. Newman's Essay* (1850).

Butt, Thomas, *Observation on Primitive Tradition and its Connexion with Evangelical Truth* (1837).

Campbell, George (1719–96), *On Miracles* (1823).

Cardwell, Edward (1787–1861), *Documentary Annals of the Reformed Church of England, being a Collection of Injunctions, Declarations, Orders, Articles of Inquiry etc.*, I–II (1839).

— *The Two Books of Common Prayer set forth by Authority of Parliament in the Reign of King Edward VI* (1841).

— *A history of the Conferences and Other Proceedings connected with the Revision of the Book of Common Prayer 1558–1690* (1841).

— Synodalia, *A Collection of Articles of Religion, Canons, and Proceedings of Convocation in the Province of Canterbury 1547–1717* (1842).

Chillingworth, William (1602–44), *The Religion of Protestants a Safe Way to Salvation, etc.* (1664).

Churton, Edward, *The Church of England a Witness and Keeper of the Catholic Tradition* (1835).

Comber, Thomas (1575–1654), *Works*, I–VII (1841).

Durel, John (1625–83), *The Liturgy of the Church of England* (1662).

Field, Richard (1561–1616), *Of the Church*, I–V (1843).

Froude, Richard Hurrell (1803–36), *Remains*, I–II (1838).

Gunning, Peter (1614–48), *Sermons* (1665).

Hales, John (1584–1656), *Golden Remains of the Ever Memorable Mr. John Hales* (1711).

Hammond, Henry (1605–60), *Works*, I–IV (1674).

Hawkins, Edward (1789–1882), *A Dissertation upon the Use and Importance of Unauthoritative Tradition* (1819).

— *An Inquiry into the Connected Uses of the Principal Means of Attaining Christian Truth* (1840).

Hey, John (1734–1815), *Lectures in Divinity*, I–IV (1822).

Holden, George (1783–1865), *The Authority of Tradition in Matters of Religion* (1838).

Hook, Walter Farquhar, *Five Sermons Preached before the University of Oxford* (1837).

Hooker, Richard (1554–1600), *The Works of that Learned and Judicious Divine Mr. Richard Hooker, with an Account of his Life and Death by Isaac Walton*, I–III (1836).

Horsley, Samuel (1733–1803), *Works*, I–VII (1812).

Jenkin, Robert (1656–1727), *The Reasonableness and Certainty of the Christian Religion* (1706).

Jewel, John (1522–71), *Apologia Ecclesiae Anglicanae* (1812).

Jones of Nayland, William (1726–1800), *Theological and Miscellaneous Works*, I–VII (1826).

Keble, John (1792–1866), *Primitive Tradition Recognized in Holy Scripture* (1839).

Laud, William (1573–1645), *A Relation of the Conference between William Laud and Mr. Fisher the Jesuit* (1639).

Leslie, Charles (1650–1722), *The Theological Works*, I–VII (1832).

Milton, John (1608–74), *De Doctrina Christiana* (1828).

More, Paul Elmer, and Frank Leslie Cross, *Anglicanism, The Thought and Practice of the Church of England, illustrated from the Religious Literature of the Seventeenth Century* (1951).

Overall, John (1560–1619), *The Convocation Book of 1606* (1844).

Paley, William (1742–1805), *Works*, I–III (1825).

Palmer, William (1803–85), *A Treatise on the Church of Christ*, I–II (1838).

Payne, William (1650–96), *The Notes of the Church as laid down by Cardinal Bellarmine, Examined and Confuted* (1687).

Pearson, John (1613–86), *An Exposition of the Creed* (1723).

Perceval, Arthur Philip (1799–1853), *An Apology for the Doctrine of Apostolical Succession* (1839).

Secker, Thomas (1693–1768), *Works*, I–VI (1771).

Shuttleworth, Philip N. (1782–1842), *Not Tradition, but Revelation* (1838).

South, Robert (1634–1716), *Sermons Preached on Several Occasions*, I–V (1842).

Stillingfleet, Edward (1635–99), *A Rational Account of the Grounds of*

Protestant Religion, being a Vindication of the Lord Archbishop of Canterbury's Relation of a Conference from the Pretended Answer by T. C. (1681).

Taylor, Jeremy (1613–67), *The Whole Works*, I–XV (1828).

Thorndike, Herbert (1598–1672), *Of the Government of Churches, a Discourse pointing at the Primitive Form* (1841).

— *The Theological Works* (1844).

Tillotson, John (1630–94), *Works*, I–X (1820).

Ussher, James (1581–1656), *Britannicarum Ecclesiarum Antiquitates* (1687).

— *De Romanae Ecclesiae Symbolo Apostolico* (1660).

— *Answer to a Jesuit, with Other Tracts on Popery* (1835).

Vincentius of Lirin's Commentary with Preface from Bishop Beveridge and a Catena of English Fathers (1837).

Warburton, William (1598–1678), *Works*, I–XII (1811).

Waterland, Daniel (1683–1740), *Works*, I–X (1823).

Whiston, William (1667–1752), *Primitive Christianity Revived*, I–IV (1711).

Whitby, Daniel (1638–1726), Δὸς ποῦ στῶ *Or, An Answer to Sure Footing* (1723).

White, Francis (1564?–1638), *A Treatise of the Sabbath Day* (1635).

Wilson, William, *A Brief Examination of Professor Keble's Visitation Sermon* (1837).

Wordsworth, Christopher (1807–85), *Letters to M. Gondon* (1847).

II. Literature

a) General

Church, R. W., *The Oxford Movement, 1833–45* (1932).

Cross, F. L., *The Oxford Dictionary of the Christian Church* (1957).

Dawson, C., *The Spirit of the Oxford Movement* (1945).

Elliot-Binns, L. E., *English Thought, 1860–1900. The Theological Aspect* (1956).

— *The Development of English Theology in the Later Nineteenth Century* (1952).

Fairbairn, A. M., *Catholicism, Roman and Anglican* (1899).

Hocedez, E., *Histoire de la Théologie au XIX siécle*, 3 vols. (1947–52).

Mackey, J. P., *The Modern Theology of Tradition* (1963).

Moran, G., *Scripture and Tradition. A Survey of the Controversy* (1963).

Newman, A. H., "Englische Theologie des 19. Jahrhunderts" in *Realenzyklopädie für protestantische Theologie und Kirche* 13 (1915), pp. 401–25.

Storr, V. F., *The Development of English Theology during the Nineteenth Century, 1800–60* (1913).

b) On John Henry Cardinal Newman

For a fuller bibliography, see *Newman-Studien*, I, pp. 301–26, II, pp. 327–43, and III, pp. 293–8.

Artz, J., "Newman und die Intuition" in *Theologische Quartalschrift* 136 (1956), pp. 174–98.

— *Glaubensbegründung aus dem Persönlichen* (1958).

— "Die Eigenständigkeit der Erkenntnistheorie John Henry Newmans" in *Theologische Quartalschrift* 139 (1959), pp. 194–222.

Barton, J. M. T., "Newman's Scriptural Studies. Liberation from a Myth" in *The Tablet* (1953), pp. 421–2.

Bastable, J. D., "Cardinal Newman's Philosophy of Belief" in *Irish Ecclesiastical Record* 83 (1955), pp. 241–52, 346–51, 436–44.

Beckmann, J. F., "Another View of Newman" in *The American Ecclesiastical Review* (1958), pp. 37–48.

Biemer, G., "The Anglican Response to Newman?" in *Philosophical Studies* 8 (1958), pp. 64–70.

— "Die Tagebücher des Kardinals" in *Oberrheinisches Pastoralblatt* 61 (1960), pp. 45–50.

— "Traditio et Scriptura iuxta Anglicanos et Card. Newman", in C. Balić, ed., *De Scriptura et Traditione* (1963), pp. 573–87.

Blehl, V., "The Holiness of John Henry Newman" in *The Month* 19 (1958), pp. 325–34.

Boekraad, A. J., "Newman en de H. Schrift" in *Streven* 7 (1954), pp. 385–8.

— *The Personal Conquest of Truth according to John Henry Newman* (1955).

Bouyer, L., *Newman, Sa vie et spiritualité* (1953); English translation: *Newman, His Life and His Spirituality* (1958).

Brunner, A., "*Idee und Entwicklung bei Hegel und Newman*" in *Scholastik* 32 (1957), pp. 1–26.

van den Bussche, H., "Newman en de Bijbel" in *Collationes Gandavenses* (1954), pp. 290–9.

Byrne, J. J., "The Notion of Doctrinal Development in the Anglican Writings of John Henry Newman" in *Ephemerides Theologicae Lovanienses* 14 (1937), pp. 230–87.

Cavallera, F., "Le Document Newman-Perrone et le développement du dogme" in *Bulletin de Littérature ecclésiastique* 47 (1946), pp. 132–42.

Chadwick, O., *From Bossuet to Newman. The Idea of Doctrinal Development* (1957).

Davis, H. F., "Was Newman a Disciple of Coleridge?" in *Dublin Review* (1945), pp. 155–72.

— "Newman's Cause" in *Blackfriars* (Offprint, 1952).

— "Newman, the Bible and the Obiter Dicta" in *The Life of the Spirit* 8 (1945), pp. 398–407.

— "Is Newman's Theory of Development Catholic?" in *Blackfriars* (1958), pp. 310–21.

Dessain, C. S., "Cardinal Newman on the Theory and Practice of Knowledge. The Purpose of the Grammar of Assent" in *Downside Review* (1957), pp. 1–23.

— "Newman's First Conversion" in *Newman-Studien*, III, pp. 37–53.

Dibble, R. A., *John Henry Newman. The Concept of Infallible Doctrinal Authority* (1955).

Dick, K., *Das Prinzip der Analogie bei Butler und Newman*. Unprinted dissertation, Munich (1958).

Fenton, J. C., "Some Newman Autobiographical Sketches and the Newman Legend" in *The American Ecclesiastical Review* 136 (1957), pp. 349–410.

— "Newman's Complaints Examined in the Light of Priestly Spirituality" in *The American Ecclesiastical Review* 138 (1958), pp. 49–65.

Fries, H., *Die Religionsphilosophie Newmans* (1948).

— "Die Dogmengeschichte des 5. Jahrhunderts im theologischen Werdegang von John Henry Newman" in A. Grillmeier and H. Borcht, ed., *Das Konzil von Chalkedon* (1954), III, pp. 421–54.

— "John Henry Newmans Weg zur Katholischen Kirche" in *Religiöse Quellenschriften* 13 (1958).

— "J. H. Newmans Beitrag zum Verständnis der Tradition" in M. Schmaus, ed., *Die mündliche Überlieferung* (1957), pp. 63–122.

Guitton, J., *La Philosophie de Newman. Essai sur l'idée du Développement* (1933).

Gorce, D., *Newman et les Pères* (1947).

Harrold, C. F., *John Henry Newman* (1955).

Johnson, J. T., "Leo XIII, Cardinal Newman and the Inerrancy of Scripture" in *Downside Review* (1951), pp. 411–27.

Karrer O., *J. H. Newman, Die Kirche. Übertragung und Einführung von O. Karrer* (2 vols., 1945–46).

Kerrigan, A., "More about Newman? An Important Contribution to the History of Scriptural Exegesis" in *Irish Ecclesiastical Record* 81 (1954), pp. 422–35.

Läpple, A., *Der Einzelne in der Kirche. Wesenszüge einer Theologie des Einzelnen nach J. H. Kardinal Newman* (1952).

Léonard, A., "La foi principe fondamental du développement du dogme" in *Revue des Sciences Philosophiques et Théologiques* 42 (1948), pp. 276–86.

May, L., *Cardinal Newman* (1945).

SELECT BIBLIOGRAPHY

Middleton, R. D., *Newman at Oxford. His Religious Development* (1950).

Nédoncelle, M., *La Philosophie religieuse de John Henry Newman* (1946).

— "Newman et le développement dogmatique" in *Revue des Sciences Religieuses* 32 (1958), pp. 197–213.

Nigg, W., "John Henry Newman" in *Prophetische Denker* (1957), pp. 129–222.

O'Dwyer, L., "Tum illud opusculum" in *Revue Théologique* 40 (1908), pp. 419–20.

O'Faolain, S., *Newman's Way. Biography* (1952).

O'Flynn, J. A., "Newman and the Scripture" in *Irish Theological Quarterly* 21 (1954), pp. 264–9.

Parkinson, H. J., *Some Centenary Addresses on Newman's Idea of a University* (1954).

Pol, H. W. van de, *Die Kirche im Leben und Denken Newmans* (1937).

Pucelle, J., "L'idéalisme et la théologie de l'Incarnation dans la pensée du XIXe siècle. F. D. Maurice, J. Martineau, J. H. Newman" in *Revue de Théologie et de Philosophie* 3 (1953), pp. 172–82.

Rickaby, J., *Index to the Works of John Henry Newman* (1914).

Reardon, B. M. G., "Newman and the Psychology of Belief" in *Church Quarterly Review* 158 (1954), pp. 315–32.

Robertson, Th. L., "The Kingsley-Newman Controversy and the Apology" in *Modern Language Notes*, 69 (1954), pp. 564–9.

Robinson, J., "Newman's Use of Butler's Arguments" in *Downside Review* 76 (1955), pp. 161–80.

Schiffers, N., *Die Einheit der Kirche nach John Henry Newman* (1956).

Seynaeve, J., *Cardinal Newman's Doctrine on Holy Scripture according to his Published Works and Previously Unedited Manuscripts* (1953).

— "Newman. Doctrine scripturaire du Cardinal" in *Dictionnaire de la Bible, Supplément* (1928 ff.), fasc. XXXI, pp. 427–74.

Smet, W. de, *De invloed van Butlers "Analogy of Religion" op Keble en Newman* (1955).

Stroeber, R., *Die Idee der Kirche von T. S. Coleridge bis John Henry Newman.* Unprinted dissertation, Erlangen (1952).

Theis, N., "Newman und die Bibel" in *Beilagen zum kirchlichen Anzeiger* (1955), pp. 27–30, 42–45, 55–62.

Tristram, H., "In the Lists with the Abbé Jager" in *Centenary Essay* (1954), pp. 201–22.

Walgrave, J. H., "Newman aan de Leuvense Alma Mater" in *Kultur-leven* 21 (1954), pp. 207–13.

— *Newman. Le Développement du Dogme* (1957).

— "Newman en de idee der doctrinele ontwikkeling" in *Tijdschrif voor Philosophie* 20 (1958), pp. 510–19.

— *Newman the Theologian* (1964).

Ward, M., *Young Mr. Newman* (1952).

Ward, W., *The Life of John Henry Cardinal Newman*, 2 vols. (1912).

Wiseman, N., *Dissertazione sullo stato attuale del protestantismo in Inghilterra* (1837).

Zeno, OFM, *Our Way to Certitude. An Introduction to Newman's Psychological Discovery: The Illative Sense and his Grammar of Assent* (1957).

INDEX OF NAMES

Adam, K., 134.
Alphonsus Liguori, 162.
Algermissen, K., 103, 110.
Allies, T. W., 38.
Ambrose, 50.
Anastasius of Antioch, 161.
Anthony, 178.
Aquinas, see Thomas Aquinas
Aristotle, 61, 62.
Arius, 90.
Arnold, F. X., 71.
Artz, J., 146.
Asmussen, H., 164.
Athanasius, 90, 161.
Atterbury, F., 10, 11.
Augustine, 161.

Baader, F. von, 125.
Bacht, H., 126, 129, 130.
Barrow, I., 17, 21.
Basil the Great, 161.
Bellarmine, Robert, 44, 100, 104, 111.
Betz, J., 71.
Biemer, G., xvii, 1, 2, 165.
Böckle, F., 152.
Blackstone, W., 172.
Bossuet, J. B., 48, 50.
Bouyer, L., 150.

Bramhall, J., 20, 36.
Breucha, H., 117.
Bull, G., 8.
Burnet, G., 13.
Burton, E., 75.
Butler, J., 11, 14, 15, 53, 74, 122
Butt, T., 28, 42.

Campbell, G., 23.
Cano, Melchior, 107.
Cardwell, E., 27.
Chadwick, O., 48, 50, 122, 124.
Chillingworth, W., 9, 14, 22.
Chrysostom, John, 9, 161.
Churton, E., 25.
Clement of Alexandria, 83, 102, 151.
Comber, T., 18.
Constantine, 75.
Conybeare, J., 10.
Cornelius a Lapide, 162.
Coulson, J., 40.
Cross, F. L., 5.
Cyprian, 162.
Cyfil of Jerusalem, 161.

Davis, H. F., xx, 34, 80, 131, 153, 169.

Dawson, C., 50.
Dealtry, W., 40.
Dessain, C. S., xx.
Dick, K., 74.
Didymus, 178.
Döllinger, I., 134.
Durel, J., 18, 19.

Elliott-Binns, L. E., 130.

Faber, F. W., 66.
Fairbairn, P., 136.
Falkland, Lord, 9.
Fausset, 135.
Feiner, J., 152.
Field, R., 19.
Fisher the Jesuit (John Fisher), 8.
Flanagan, J. S., 59, 65, 108, 131, 143, 169.
Francis de Sales, 117.
Fries, H., xviii, xix, 3, 134, 147, 155.
Froude, R. H., 25, 26, 30, 39, 46, 50, 135.

Geiselmann, J. R., 52, 69, 76, 91, 144, 161, 165, 167.
Gladstone, W. E., 26.
Gondon, M., 129.
Gunning, P., 12.

Hackney, 182.
Hadley, J. J., 106.
Haecker, T., 132.
Hales, J., 10, 22.
Hammond, H., 8, 9, 15, 20, 23, 25.
Harrison, B., 28, 43, 46.
Hawkins, E., 24, 25, 36–38, 45.
Hey, J., 13.
Hickes, G., 26.
Holden, G., 29.
Honorius, 181.

Hook, W. F., 25.
Hooker, R., 13, 16, 18.
Horsley, S., 9, 21.

Ignatius of Antioch, 44, 162.
Irenaeus, 41, 162, 178.
Isaac, S., 6.

Jager, J. N., 43, 44, 46, 47, 49, 70, 97, 101, 162.
James, W., 36.
Jenkins, D., 8, 145.
Jewel, J., 6, 13.
John Chrysostom,
    see Chrysostom, John,
John XXII, 181.
Jortin, J., 8, 11.

Karrer, O., 121, 163, 164.
Keble, J., 25, 28, 29, 33, 38, 40–42, 63, 89, 105, 157.
Kenny, T., 138.
Kuhn, J. E., 52.

Laud, W., 8, 12, 14, 15, 21, 23.
Leslie, C., 6, 11, 22.
Liguori, Alphonsus,
    see Alphonsus Liguori.
Lloyd, C., 38.
Lorinser, F., 130, 131, 139.
Lynch, T., 57.

Maher, 182.
Manning, H. E., 66.
Mayers, W., 34.
Melchior Cano,
    see Cano, Melchior.
Migne, J. P., 54.
Milton, J., 13.
Möhler, J. A., 76, 93, 101, 121.
More, P. E., 5.

INDEX OF NAMES

Mozley, A., 19, 30, 33, 39, 40, 90, 110, 163.
Murphy, J. L., 107.

Nedoncelle, M., 75.
Newman, Francis, 25.

Optatus, 161.
Origen, 161.
Overall, J., 21.

Paley, W., 7.
Palmer, W., 25, 27, 29, 30, 161.
Paul III, 181.
Payne, W., 22.
Pearson, J., 17.
Perceval, A. P., 26.
Perrone, G., 29, 30, 57, 60, 143, 169.
Pieper, J., 140.
Pius IV, 181.
Pius IX, 107, 181.
Pol, H. W. van de, 3.
Polycarp, 162.
Przywara, E., 121.
Pusey, E. B., 63, 64.

Rahner, K., 71, 124, 128.
Ranft, J., 162.
Rogers, F., 40.
Ryder, I. D., 59, 107, 123.

Salmeron, A., 162.
Schelkle, K. H., 153, 159.
Schiffers, N., 3.
Schildenberger, J., 152.
Schlier, H., 71, 131.
Schmaus, M., xviii, 69, 91, 129.
Secker, T., 6, 7, 8, 22.
Seynaeve, J., 3, 65, 128, 152, 153, 154, 155, 156, 163.
Sharp, J., 9, 10.

Shuttleworth, P. N., 29, 30.
Smyth, K., xx.
South, R., 8, 9.
Stillingfleet, E., 23.

Tavard, G. H., 2.
Taylor, J., 8, 11, 13, 19, 90.
Taymans, 122.
Tertullian, 16, 41, 161.
Theodoret, 161.
Thomas Aquinas, 97.
Thorndike, H., 16, 18.
Tillotson, J., 15.
Torquemada, Juan de, see Turrecremata, Juan de.
Tristram, H., xx, 35, 46.
Trütsch, J., 152.
Turrecremata, Juan de, 111.

Ussher, J., 13, 18.

Victoria, Queen, 26.
Vigilius, 181.
Vincent of Lerins, 41, 54, 55, 131, 134, 161.
Voisin, J. de, 46.

Walgrave, J. H., xviii, 3, 48, 129.
Warburton, W., 20.
Ward, M., 50, 125.
Ward, W., 36, 61, 62, 67, 80, 81, 136.
Ward, W. G., 59, 123.
Waterland, D., 7, 9, 12, 17.
Whately, R., 27, 36.
Whitaker, W., 18.
Whitby, D., 11, 15.
White, F., 14, 15.
Wiemann, F., 117.
Wilson, W., 28, 42.
Wiseman, N., 26.
Wordsworth, C., 129.

Zeno, 146.